AF505637

**LETTER FROM THE
SECRETARY OF THE INTERIOR**

LETTER

FROM THE

SECRETARY OF THE INTERIOR,

COMMUNICATING,

IN COMPLIANCE WITH THE RESOLUTION OF THE SENATE
OF THE 2D INSTANT, INFORMATION IN RELATION TO
THE EARLY LABORS OF THE MISSIONARIES OF
THE AMERICAN BOARD OF COMMISSIONERS
FOR FOREIGN MISSIONS IN OREGON,
COMMENCING IN 1836.

————◆•◆•◆————

WASHINGTON:
GOVERNMENT PRINTING OFFICE.
1903.

LETTER
FROM THE
SECRETARY OF THE INTERIOR

COMMUNICATING,

IN COMPLIANCE WITH THE RESOLUTION
OF THE SENATE OF THE 2D INSTANT,
INFORMATION IN RELATION
TO THE EARLY LABORS
OF THE
MISSIONARIES
OF THE AMERICAN BOARD
OF COMMISSIONERS FOR FOREIGN MISSIONS
IN OREGON, COMMENCING IN 1836.

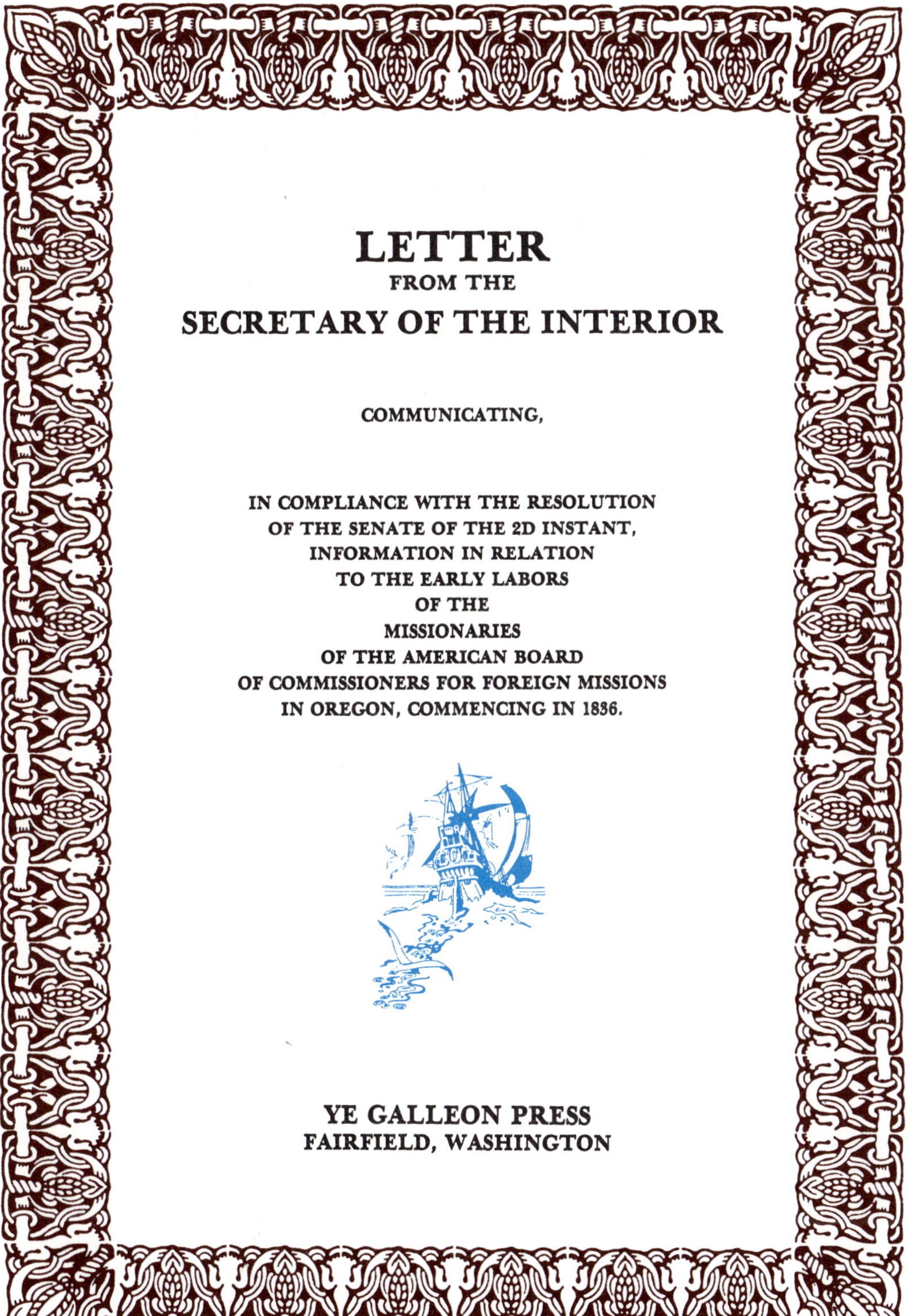

YE GALLEON PRESS
FAIRFIELD, WASHINGTON

In the Senate of the United States,
January 15, 1903.

Ordered, That there be printed for the use of the Senate two thousand five hundred additional copies of Senate Executive Document Numbered Thirty-seven, Forty-first Congress, third session, the same being a letter from the Secretary of the Interior to Honorable Schuyler Colfax, President of the Senate, of date February eight, eighteen hundred and seventy-one, directing the Secretary of the Interior to furnish any information in the possession of his Department pertaining to the "early labors of the missionaries of the American Board of Commissioners for Foreign Missions in Oregon, commencing in eighteen hundred and thirty-six."

Attest:

Charles G. Bennett, *Secretary,*
By H. M. Rose, *Chief Clerk.*

Library of Congress Cataloging-in-Publication Data

United States. Dept. of the Interior. Office of the Secretary.
Letter from the secretary of the interior.

Reprint. Originally published: Washington: G.P.O., 1903.

1. Whitman Massacre, 1847. 2. Indians of North America—Northwest, Pacific—Missions. I Title.

F880.U58   1988   979.5 '03   88-14285
ISBN 0-87770-451-1

LETTER

FROM

THE SECRETARY OF THE INTERIOR,

COMMUNICATING,

In compliance with the resolution of the Senate of the 2d instant, informa-tion in relation to the early labors of the missionaries of the American Board of Commissioners for Foreign Missions in Oregon, commencing in 1836.

FEBRUARY 9, 1871.—Referred to the Committee on Indian Affairs and ordered to be printed.

DEPARTMENT OF THE INTERIOR,
Washington, D. C. February 8, 1871.

SIR: In answer to a resolution of the Senate of the 2d instant, direct-ing the Secretary of the Interior to furnish any information in the pos-session of his Department pertaining to the "early labors of the mission-aries of the American Board of Commissioners for Foreign Missions in Oregon, commencing in 1836," I have the honor to transmit herewith a copy of the report of the Commissioner of Indian Affairs, dated the 6th instant, together with the documents therein referred to, which contain all the information in possession of this Department in relation to the subject.

Very respectfully, your obedient servant,

C. DELANO,
Secretary.

Hon. SCHUYLER COLFAX,
President of the Senate.

DEPARTMENT OF THE INTERIOR,
OFFICE OF INDIAN AFFAIRS,
Washington, D. C., February 6, 1871.

SIR: I have the honor to acknowledge the receipt, by reference from your Department, of Senate resolution dated the 2d instant, calling for information in regard to the early labors of missionaries of the American Board of Commissioners for Foreign Missions in Oregon, and respect-fully, in answer to your direction for a report in the matter, to say that the desired information will no doubt be found in the documents fur-nished by Dr. H. H. Spalding to A. B. Meacham, superintendent of Indian affairs, submitted by the latter to you on the 28th ultimo, and which were, with his letter, by your direction referred to this office on the 3d instant.

I herewith transmit these papers as being all that are on file in this office relating to the subject.

Very respectfully, your obedient servant,

E. S. PARKER,
Commissioner.

Hon. C. DELANO,
Secretary of the Interior.

WASHINGTON, *January* 28, 1871.

SIR: I am respectfully requested by the Rev. H. H. Spalding, the oldest living Protestant missionary in Oregon, to place on file in your Department the accompanying documents giving a history of the early missionary work and labors of Dr. Marcus Whitman, himself, and others; the progress and civilization of the Indians under their charge, without aid from the Government; also a history of the massacre of Dr. Whitman and others; also resolutions of Christian associations in answer to Executive Document No. 38, House of Representatives, and a variety of historical information which it would seem proper to have on file or placed in some more permanent form of future history, that our people upon the Pacific as well as the Atlantic coast may be reminded of the self-sacrificing dispositions of these early missionaries, as well as their patriotic devotion to our country, which, in so great a measure, led to the acquisition of that vast territory upon the Pacific coast. All of which is respectfully submitted.

A. B. MECHAM,
Superintendent Indian Affairs, Oregon.

Hon. COLUMBUS DELANO,
Secretary of the Interior.

THE EARLY LABORS OF THE MISSIONARIES OF THE AMERICAN BOARD OF COMMISSIONERS FOR FOREIGN MISSIONS IN OREGON, COMMENCING IN 1836, AND OTHER DOCUMENTS PERTAINING TO THE SAME.

HISTORY OF MISSIONS ON THE NORTHWEST COAST.

THE SUCCESS OF MISSIONS THE WEALTH OF THE NATION—OREGON SAVED BY THEM TO THE PEOPLE OF THE UNITED STATES—THE MISSIONARY, THE PATRIOT THE MARTYR—THE TWO AMERICAN HEROINES OF THE NINETEENTH CENTURY—THE AMERICAN WOMAN AND THE BRITISH LION—WHAT WOMAN HAS DONE TO DEVELOP A CONTINENT.

In presenting this history to the people of the United States, we will glance—

1st. At the Oregon of 1834, the date that marks the first successful enterprise to secure to the people of the United States their vast Territories west of the Rocky Mountains—its dreary and worthless character, as regarded even by our Government, by reason of its supposed desolate character, and its remoteness and inaccessibility by land route.

2d. The helpless condition of the Territory at that date, in the hands of the Hudson's Bay Company, a powerful British monopoly, governed by a board of directors in London, with a governor and 54 sworn officers in the Territory, with 515 articled men and over 800 half-breeds and all the Indian tribes under their control, with a line of well-established and strongly-fortified posts, under strict military rule, extending from the Pacific to the Atlantic, and a complete control of this coast for 2,000 miles.

3d. The hostility of that company to the presence of American citizens in the country, and their policy to exclude American settlements, and their efforts to secure the settlement of British subjects, although by the treaty renewed three times by said governments the American citizen had the same right with the British subject.

4th. The early Oregon missions, their importance in securing the country to Americans, by demonstrating the practicability of an emigrant route across the continent; by communicating to the people of the United States important information concerning the country; by establishing schools and laying the foundations of civilized society in the valley of the Willamette, and doing much to bring forward the provisional government; but especially by the herculean labors of the martyr Whitman through the winter snows of the Rocky Mountains, to reach the city of Washington and to communicate to the Government the certainty of a wagon route, and the value of the country, by which its cession to Great Britain was prevented; and by his successfully bringing through, in 1843, that emigration of nearly 1,000 souls, with their wagons, to the Columbia.

5th. The Whitman massacre and the attempt to break up the American settlements.

6th. Who excited the Indians to murder the Americans?

7th. What do the citizens of Oregon and Washington think of Executive Document No. 38?

8th. What is expected of Congress?

I.—THE OREGON OF 1834.

We had a right to Oregon, first by discovery of the Columbia River; second, we had the right of possession by purchase of all the territory west of the Mississippi, claimed as Louisiana by France, and purchased by Jefferson in 1804. Had that failed we had the right of possession by purchase of Spain, in 1819, of all their possessions gained by discovery, or in any other way, north of 42° north latitude, so that we had a three-fold right as stated by Webster. But possession by right is very different from possession in fact. Gentlemen present are aware that that region, for a long time, was a *terra incognita* to most of the business world. The Hudson's Bay Company at length crowded out, not only the Northwest Company's posts, but Mr. Astor's also, and changed the name of Astoria to Fort George, thus gaining complete possession.—*Address of Dr. Atkinson, of Portland, before the New York Chamber of Commerce, December,* 1868.

At that time, however, the gloom of desolation hung like a pall over these regions. Many of you can recall the dread in those times of the North Pacific Coast and its imagined dreary and dreamy loneliness. The unfortunate result of Astor's Columbia River project, the fate of the Tonquin, Jewett's narrative of the wreck and capture of the ship Boston and her crew, especially the terrible work of death by starvation and hardships among Wilson G. Hunt's party, had stripped the northwest coast of America of a single inviting feature. But in a greater degree the immortal Bryant, in his 'Vision of Death,' dedicated these shores as its fit abiding place, and presents the grim monster as penetrating these

> "Continuous woods.
> Where rolls the Oregon, and hears no sound
> Save its own dashings."

He then breaks the awful silence of his own creation in the oracular assurance,

> "Yet the dead are there."

The education of an American youth, in those days, was thought to have been neglected if he were unable to recite those memorable verses. Have you not felt the contagion of that inspiration? Are you not, even now, sometimes affected by that ideality? Transfer yourselves to your Atlantic homes, and imagine these ocean-washed shores, these immense mountain chains, our high northern latitude and proximity to the polar regions; regain once more your ideal conception of the remoteness of West from East, and then couple with these thoughts, 'Yet the dead are there.' Much as I love the poetry, greatly as I admire the venerable bard who has given such prestige to American literature, yet how cruel was he to the home of my adoption. Methinks he stamped on the region the grim idea of its fitness for a charnel house. Will you risk life there, for it may be your lot, out of the presence and far removed from all you hold dear, there to fall alone, unwept and unmourned? Will you take mother, wife, sister, child, to such a place? That sublime composition made me, when a schoolboy, imagine this northwest coast and the mighty Columbia the dreamiest and most inhospitable of earth. An idea, whether just or unjust, molds the history of passing events. That one surely passed into history, and impressed Oregon with a solitude so profound, it were almost sacrilege in men to attempt to disturb. So, at least, seemed to believe the American Government, and many leading American statesmen, for nearly half a century; and although two American women set the example by which the presence here of thousands of men, women, and children, should have dissipated this spell, yet still it clings to the region like the fabled shirt of Nessus, and even now the great Northern Pacific Railroad incurs its greatest hostility, because those who never visited these shores can not appreciate the vast importance, resources, and desirability of Northwest America. So with the weapon of groundless prejudice, *soi disant* statesmen damnify the country, and call the shortest route across the American continent within the United States, clearest of obstacles and freest from obstruction by snows, a Siberian trail. These are the curiosities of our history, endowing it with a lively interest.—*Hon. Edward Evans.*

II.—THE HELPLESS CONDITION OF THE TERRITORY, AT THAT DATE, IN THE HANDS OF THE HUDSON'S BAY COMPANY.

Senator Benton, in 1825, when the joint occupancy was before the Senate:

"The claim of Great Britain was nothing but a naked pretension, founded on the double purpose of benefiting herself and of injuring the United States. That fur-trader, Sir Alexander McKenzie, is at the bottom of this policy. Failing in his attempt to explore the Columbia River in 1793, he nevertheless urged upon the British government the advantages of taking it to herself and of expelling the Americans from the whole region west of the Rocky Mountains. He recommended that the Hudson's Bay Company and the Northwest Company should be united, and they have been; he proposed to extend the fur trade to the Pacific shores, and it has been so extended; he proposed that a chain of posts should be formed from sea to sea, and it has been done; he recommended that no boundary line should be formed which did not give the Columbia River to the British, and the British ministry declare that none other shall be formed; he proposed to obtain command of the fur trade from latitude 45° north, and they have it even to the Mandan villages and the Council Bluffs; he recommended the expulsion of the American fur-traders from the whole region west of the Rocky Mountains, and they are excluded from it."

Sir James Douglass's testimony, given in answer to interrogatory 11, in the case of The Hudson's Bay Company's Claim *vs.* United States:

"The honorable Hudson's Bay Company had fifty-five officers and five hundred and fifteen articled men. The company, having a large, active, and experienced force of servants in their employ, and holding establishments judiciously situated in the most favorable portions for trade, forming, as it were, a network of posts, aiding and supporting each other, possessed an extraordinary influence with the natives, and in 1846 practically enjoyed a monopoly in the fur trade in the country west of the Rocky Mountains north and south of the forty-ninth parallel of latitude. The profits of their trade from 1841 to 1846 were at least seven thousand pounds sterling annually— about $35,000."

III.—HOSTILITY OF THE HUDSON'S BAY COMPANY TO AMERICAN CITIZENS.

Swan's work, 1852, page 381:

"The officers of the company also sympathized with their servants, and a deadly feeling of hatred has existed between these officers and the American emigrants, in coming across the mountains to squat upon lands they considered theirs; and there is not a man among them who would not be glad to have had every American emigrant driven out of the country."

Fitz Gerald on the Hudson's Bay Company, before the British Parliament, in 1849:

"A corporation who, under authority of a charter which is invalid in law, hold a monopoly in commerce and exercise a despotism in government, and have so exercised that monopoly and so wielded that power as to shut up the earth from the knowledge of man and man from the knowledge of God."

Sir George Simpson, in his "History Around the World," fore part of 1847:

"I defy the American Congress to establish their Atlantic tariff in the Pacific ports."

General Brouilett's "Protestanism in Oregon," p. 51 of the edition published by order of the House of Representatives, says:

"The massacre at Waiilatpu has not been committed by the Indians in hatred of heretics If Americans only have been killed, it is only because the war had been declared by the Indians against the Americans only, and not against foreigners; and it was in their quality as American citizens, and not as Protestants, that the Indians killed them."

Senator Benton, before the Senate, May, 1848, urging Government to extend its arm of protection over Oregon Territory, in answer to the urgent call of the citizens after the Waiilatpu tragedy:

"But which has had the effect of depriving those people of all government and of bringing about the massacres which have taken place, in which the benevolent missionary has fallen in the midst of his labors."

IV.—THE EARLY OREGON MISSIONS—THEIR IMPORTANCE IN SECURING THE COUNTRY TO THE AMERICANS.

'mmediately on the appearance of said Executive Document No. 38, of the Thirty-
 h Congress, though long after its publication, a committee was appointed at a pub-
 . meeting in Linn County, Oregon, to investigate said document, with power to send
 r documents and to collect testimony; they immediately addressed a circular of ques-
 ns to many old Oregonians, officers, civil and military, and to the surviving captives
 d sufferers of the Whitman massacre and the Indian wars that followed. A great
 nount of valuable testimony has thus been collected, completely refuting the charges
made in said document under the strange heading, "Protestantism in Oregon,"
against the early pioneers of Oregon.

We can give only extracts from the great mass of historic facts:

Question.—Do you believe, from your long acquaintance with the Nez Perces and Cayuse Indians, that the Protestant missions established among them in 1836 were productive of good both in elevating the natives from the wretched condition of want and ignorance of letters, of cultivation, and of God, in which the missionaries found them, to a comparatively high state of civilization and Christain attainments; as also in securing the constant friendship and firm alliance of the Nez Perces nation to the Americans and the American Government?

Answers.—I certainly do. I firmly believe that the instructions the Nez Perces received from their missionaries kept them from joining in the wars against the Americans.

GEO. ABERNATHY,
Ex-Governor of the Territory of Oregon, 1845–'49.

I answer most emphatically yes; and have so expressed myself in my history and on all occasions.

JOEL PALMER.

[Palmer was commissary general in the Cayuse war, well acquainted with Whitman and Spalding and their labors; superintendent of Indian affairs for those tribes, and member of the Oregon legislature.]

I arrived in this country in 1839, and from personal knowledge I answer yes.

J. S. GRIFFIN.

I arrived in this country in 1839, and from personal knowlegde I answer yes.

WM. GEIGER.

The condition of the savages (Cayuse) has been greatly ameliorated, and their improvement is attributable to the missionary residents (p. 57). Mr. and Mrs. Spalding have kept up a school and many of the Indians have made great proficiency. The Nez Perces are a quiet and industrious people, and owe much of their superior qualifications to the missionaries. In this lonely situation they (Mr. and Mrs. Spalding) have spent the best of their days for no other compensation than a scanty subsistence.—*Palmer's History,* pages 128, 131.

This is evidently the most promising Indian mission in Oregon. I would here take occasion to observe that the Rev. H. H. Spalding and his heroic companion are laboring faithfully both for the spiritual and temporal good of this people (Nez Perces), and in no part of the world have I seen more visible fruits of labor thus bestowed. Far away from all civilized society, and depending for their safety from the fury of excited savages alone in the protection of Heaven, they are entitled to the sympathy and prayers of the whole Christian church.—*Hines's History Around the World,* page 172.

Through the self-abnegating labors of this good old man (Spalding) these aborigines, we feel safe in saying, have been benefited more than by all the thousands of outlay by the Government. Their savage natures are changed in his presence, and from the chiefs to the humblest they obey and reverence him as do dutiful children a parent.—*Golden Age, Lewiston, Idaho Territory, November,* 16, 1864.

We concur in the above.

JOEL PALMER.
GEO. ABERNATHY.

[Extracts from Commodore Wilkes.]

Vol. IV, page 460: "He (Spalding) has not neglected to attend to the proper sphere of his duties, for his labors in this respect will compare with those of his brethren. * * His efforts in agriculture are not less exemplary. * * The Indians, have a strong desire for cattle. A party was persuaded to accompany a missionary over the Rocky Mountains, and take horses to the States to exchange for cattle, but they were destroyed by the Sioux. * * Among the other duties of Mr. Spalding, he has taught them the art of cultivation, and many of them have plantations; these are kept in good order. * * Mr. Spalding kindly loans them his plows and other implements, and on a difficulty arising among them he has only to threaten them with the loss of the plow to bring the refractory persons to reason. * * The women are represented as coming miles to learn to knit, spin, and weave, and to assist Mrs. Spalding in her large school and domestic avocations. * * The great endeavor of Mr. Spalding is to induce the Indians to give up their roving mode of life, and to settle down, and cultivate the soil, and in this he is succeeding admirably. He shows admirable tact and skill, together with untiring industry and perseverance, in the prosecution of his labors as a missionary; and he appears to be determined to leave nothing undone that one person alone can perform. * * In the winter the time of himself and that of his wife is devoted to teaching, at which season their school is much enlarged. * * Our gentlemen heard the pupils read. In the winter the school at the station numbers about five hundred scholars, but in the summer not one-tenth of that number attend."—*Wilkes's Exploring Expedition around the World during the years* 1840, '41, '42, '43. Vol. 4, pages 460-465.

I concur in the above statements.

GEO. ABERNATHY.

I heartily concur in the above.

JOEL PALMER.

We concur in the above.

J. S. GRIFFIN.
WM. GEIGER.

CENTERVILLE, OREGON, *December*, 14, 1868.

DEAR SIR: I have seen and read with pleasure a memorial signed by Edward R. Geary and others, a committee appointed by the Oregon Presbytery of the Old School, and the United Presbyterian Churches, to devise measures for the renewal of the work of Christian missions among the nation of the Nez Perces Indians, and to reinstate the Rev. H. H. Spalding. * * I most heartily concur in the statements therein contained, and earnestly recommend that your excellency appoint Rev. H. H. Spalding superintendent of instruction. * * I have been acquainted with Mr. Spalding ever since 1845, and am personally knowing to most of the facts set forth in the memorial. I was in that country during the Cayuse war in 1848. And then, again, in 1855 and 1856, I commanded the Oregon volunteers, when there was a concert of action among all the Indian tribes on our northwest coast, except the Nez Perces alone, who, as a tribe, have always been friendly to the Americans. In the spring of 1856 they furnished horses to remount a portion of the volunteers under my command, then in the valley of Walla-Walla, for the purpose of waging war against the other tribes, all of whom were hostile to the Americans south and west of the Spokans, except the Nez Perces.

In conclusion, permit me to say that I have no hesitancy in believing that the interests of the Government and that of the tribe would be better subserved by the appointment of Mr. Spalding than by any other man.

I have the honor to be, sir, very respectfully, your obedient servant,

T. R. CORNATIUS,
Former President of the Oregon Senate.

To His Excellency Governor BALLARD,
 Of the Territory of Idaho, ex-officio Superintendent of Indian Affairs.

We concur in the sentiments above expressed.

GEORGE ABERNATHY.
JOEL PALMER.
A. HINMAN.

BROWNSVILLE, *November* 4, 1868.

SIR: The undersigned ministers and members of the Willamette Presbytery of the Cumberland Presbyterian Church desire to represent that they have this day read a memorial addressed to your excellency, in behalf of the Rev. H. H. Spalding, indorsed by the Oregon Presbytery of the Old School Church, also by the Oregon Presbyteries of the United Presbyterian Church, and by the Pleasant Bute Baptist Church, and by many citizens of Linn County and vicinity, where said Spalding has been longest and best known.

It affords us pleasure to express our hearty concurrence in the sentiments contained in said memorial, and further to assure you that it will be a source of deep gratification to the membership and ministers of the denomination which we represent to have the object named in the memorial effected as soon as practicable; believing that in so doing only a moiety of justice would be done to a worthy and good man, and to one who has labored and suffered more for this Pacific coast than any other living man.

Very respectfully, your obedient servants,

W. R. BISHOP,
LUTHER WHITE,
Committee of Presbytery.

D. W. BALLARD,
Governor and ex-officio Superintendent of Indian Affairs for Idaho Territory.

LEWISTON, *February 22, 1865.*

SIR: I was United States Indian agent in charge of the Nez Perces Nation, Idaho Territory, when the Rev. H. H. Spalding, who had been appointed superintendent of instruction for Nez Perces Indians by Superintendent Hale, arrived at the Lapwai agency in the fall of 1862. At the time of his arrival a great part of the tribe was collected at the agency, and I must say they seemed highly delighted at seeing Mr. Spalding again. They seemed much pleased at the idea of having a school started among them, and of having a minister who could preach to them in their own language.

Every Sabbath the Indians in great numbers attended Mr. Spalding's preaching, and I was greatly astonished at the orderly and dignified deportment of the congregation. Although Mr. Spalding had been absent from the tribe many years, yet they retained all the forms of worship that he had taught them. Many of them have prayers night and morning in their lodges. The Nez Perces have always maintained friendly relations with the Americans. This is, no doubt, in a great measure to be attributed to the influence and teachings of Mr. Spalding. In my opinion, Mr. Spalding, by his own personal labors, has accomplished more good in this tribe than all the money expended by Government has been able to effect. Not having any suitable school-house, I permitted Mr. Spalding to open his school in my office shortly after his arrival, and from that time till he was compelled to discontinue the school from severe sickness, the office was crowded not only with children, but with old men and women, some compelled to use glasses to assist their sight. Some of the old men would remain till bed-time engaged in transcribing into their language portions of Scripture translated by Mr. Spalding. The desire I have to correct any false impression that may have gone abroad with regard to the reception of Mr. Spalding by the tribe on his return to the Lapwai in the fall of 1862, is the only apology I will offer for troubling you with this communication.

I remain, very respectfully, your obedient servant,

J. W. ANDERSON.

I concur.

G. ABERNATHY.

I concur.

JOEL PALMER.

S. H. ATKINS, D. D.

[From the Pacific, San Francisco, California, February 6, 1864.]

On Sunday last I had the pleasure of attending church at this place. The services were conducted in the Nez Perces language by the Rev. H. H. Spalding, who came to this people with his heroic wife in 1836.

The governor of the Territory was present, and all the Federal officers and nearly all the county officers, with most of the citizens of Lewiston. The large court-room was crowded to its utmost capacity. The scene was deeply solemn and interesting; the breathless silence, the earnest, devout attention of that great Indian congregation (even the small child) to the words of their much-loved pastor; the spirit, the sweet melody of their singing, the readiness with which they turned to hymns and chapters, and read with Mr. Spalding the Sabbath lessons from their Testaments, which Mr. Spalding had translated and printed twenty years before; the earnest, pathetic voice of the native Christians whom Mr. Spalding called upon to pray—all, all, deeply and solemnly impressed that large congregation of white spectators even to tears. It would be better to-day, a thousand times over, if Government would do away with its policy that is so inefficiently carried out, and only lend its aid to a few such men as Mr. Spalding, whose whole heart is in the business, who has but one desire, and that to civilize and christianize these Indians. To-day shows what can be done when the heart is right.

ALEX. SMITH,
Judge First Judicial District, Territory of Idaho.

I concur.

GEORGE ABERNATHY.

I heartily concur.

JOEL PALMER.

I heartily concur.

A. HINMAN.

From Hon. D. S. Thompson, of Oregon Senate.

WASHINGTON, D. C., *January* 20, 1871.

DEAR SIR: I was employed during the past summer in surveying into twenty-acre lots a part of the Nez Perces reservation, Idaho Territory. I have been in the western portion of the United States, among the Indians, the greatest portion of my life, and I believe the Nez Perces Indians are by far the most intelligent and susceptible of civilization of any Indians of which I am acquainted. The work done by yourself for these Indians, years ago, you must feel yourself well paid for when you see what they now are, and what they were when you first went among them. Last year they raised not less than 50,000 bushels of wheat, 10,000 bushels of corn, 10,000 bushels of oats, besides large quantities of potatoes and other vegetables. I am rejoiced to hear that you are going back to that people; you are better acquainted with them than any other man, and I know they regard you their best friend.

  Yours, &c.,

                 D. S. THOMPSON.

  Rev. H. H. SPALDING.

[From the Chicago Advance, December 1, 1870.]

AN EVENING WITH AN OLD MISSIONARY.

One day last week a man of humble appearance, about seventy years of age, called at our office, and was introduced by a stranger as the Rev. H. H. Spalding, of Oregon. We had heard something of his labors as a missionary among the Indians in that region, and were glad to take the veteran by the hand. He was on the way to his old home at the East, after an absence of thirty-four years, and intended to stay over but a single train in Chicago. The few words we could then have together led us to press him to share our hospitalities for the night, which he accepted.

"Dr. Whitman's wife and mine," said the missionary, as we drew up our chairs about the study-table and opened our "Colton" to the right map, "were the first white women that ever crossed the Rocky Mountains. That saved Oregon to the Union. It was God's plan to give the wealth of the Pacific slope to the United States through the agency of missionaries." We asked for an explanation. "The Northwestern territory was then occupied by the Hudson's Bay Company. Who should finally possess it—England or the United States—depended upon who could first settle it with an immigration. The Hudson's Bay Company desired to secure it for their half-breeds and the Jesuits. They were slowly creeping down from Selkirk settlement, here on the north," pointing it out on the map, "and silently taking possession, with forts and trading posts. Neither wagons nor women, they industriously said, can ever pass the terrible rock-barriers that wall out Oregon from the United States. Trappers, traders, travelers, everybody echoed the words: 'No white woman can cross the mountains and live.' Seven different companies of male emigrants from the East had been shrewdly harried out of the country by their machinations. But they couldn't do it with us," said he, rising excitedly. "When the missionaries, with their wives and a wagon, appeared on the 'divide,' one of them said: 'Here is somebody that you can't get rid of so easy. These folks have come to stay.'"

"But how came you to go?" we asked. And then for four hours of the rarest interest we listened to the wonderful story. It would take a volume to unfold it. We must press it into the briefest possible space.

The Macedonian Nez Perces.—About their council fire, in solemn conclave —it was in the year 1832—the Flatheads and Nez Perces had determined to send four of their number to "the Rising Sun" for "that Book from Heaven." They had got word of the Bible and a Saviour in some way from the Iroquois. These four dusky wise men, one of them a chief, who had thus dimly "seen His star in the east," made their way to St. Louis. And it is significant of the perils of this thousand miles' journey that only one of them survived to return. They fell into the hands of General Clark, who, with Lewis, had traveled extensively in the regions of the Columbia River. He was a Romanist, and took them to his church, and, to entertain them, to the theater. How utterly he failed to meet their wants is revealed in the sad words with which they departed: "I came to you"—and the survivor repeated the words years afterward to Mr. Spalding—"with one eye partly opened; I go back with both eyes closed and both arms broken. My people sent me to obtain that Book from Heaven. You took me where your women dance as we do not allow ours to dance; and the Book was not there. You took me where I saw men worship God with candles; and the Book was not there. I am not to return without it, and my people will die in darkness." And so they took their leave. But this sad lament was overheard. A young man wrote it to his friends in Pittsburg. They showed the account to Catlin, of Indian portrait fame, who had just come from the Rocky Mountains. He said: "It cannot be; those Indians were in our company, and I heard nothing of this. Wait till I write to Clark before you publish it." He wrote. The response was: "It is true. That was the sole object of their visit— to get the Bible." Then Catlin said, "Give it to the world." The Methodists at once commissioned Rev. Mr. Lee to go and find this tribe, who had so strangely broken out of their darkness toward the light. Dr. Marcus Whitman, of the American Board, who was too late for the overland caravan for that summer, followed the next year. Lee found the Nez Perces; but so fearful were the ridges and the ravines of the path to them, and so wild the country where they roamed, that the gift of ten horses, with which they pleaded their cause, could not keep him. He pushed on to the tribes living near the coast, and sent for his wife and associates by the way of Cape Horn.

Woman's heroism.—It was with great joy the Nez Perces welcomed Whitman the next year. Having explored the situation, and taking with him two boys, which the Indians had placed in his hands as hostages, in some sort, for his return, he went back for his intended wife, and to secure others for the work. But who would go? Men could be found; but where was the woman willing to brave the vague horrors of that "howling wilderness?" His betrothed consented. But an associate, and he a married man, must be obtained. More than a score of most devoted ones were applied to in vain. Friends said, "It is madness to make the attempt." And we do not wonder; for that country, and the way between, in the popular impression, was a dark unknown, full of terrors.

The dead are there where rolls the Oregon,

wrote Bryant. The dead were there, and the bones of not a few luckless emigrants strewed the path to the mountains.

A year was spent in the search for associates, and then light came from an unexpected quarter. In the early spring of 1836 a sleigh, extemporized from a wagon, was crunching through the deep snows of western New York. It contained Rev. Mr. and Mrs. Spalding, who were on their way, under commission of the American Board, to the Osage Indians The wife had started from a bed of lingering illness, and was then able to walk less than a quarter of a mile.

Dr. Whitman, having heard of the rare courage of this woman, by permission of the board, started in pursuit.

"We want you for Oregon," was the hail with which he overtook them.

"How long will the journey take?"

"The summers of two years."

"What convoy shall we have?"

"The American Fur Company to the 'divide.'"

"What shall we have to live on?"

"Buffalo meat, till we can raise our own grain."

"How shall we journey?"

"On horseback."

"How cross the rivers?"

"Swim them."

After this brief dialogue—and we give it precisely in his own words—Mr. Spalding turned to his wife and said:

"My dear, my mind is made up. It is not your duty to go; but we will leave it to you after we have prayed."

By this time they had reached a tavern in the town of Howard, New York. Taking a private room, they each prayed in turn, and then left Mrs. Spalding to herself. In about ten minutes she appeared with a beaming face, and said, "I have made up my mind to go."

"But your health, my dear."

"*I like the command just as it stands.* 'Go ye into all the world,' *and no exceptions for poor health.*"

"But the perils, in your weak condition—you don't begin to think how great they are."

"The dangers of the way and the weakness of my body are His; duty is mine."

"But the Indians will take you prisoner. They are frantic for such captives. You will never see your friends again"—and the strong man broke down and began to cry.

Was it the wife that answered, or was it a voice from the old time?

"What mean ye to weep and to break mine heart? for I am ready, not to be bound only, but also to die at Jerusalem, or in the Rocky Mountains, for the name of the Lord Jesus."

"Then," said the veteran, with a charming simplicity, "I had to come to it. I didn't know anything."

"Well, you were crazy," we interposed, "to think of such a journey and she so weak."

"We were, but God meant to have us go. He wanted to have an emigration go across the mountains, and this was the way he took to start it."

Mr. and Mrs. Spalding continued their journey, and Whitman, sending forward to his bride to be ready, went back for his Indian boys—they were then about sixteen years old—and pressed on after them.   There was a hasty wedding by the way, and then the bridal tour began.

But the strife of parting was not yet over.   At Pittsburg, Cincinnati, St. Louis—all along the way—hands were stretched out to hold them back.   Catlin, at Pittsburg, assured them they could not take women through.   The hostile Indians that hover about the convoy would fight against any odds to capture them.   One woman had tried it, but the company was massacred, and she was dragged away and never heard of again.   Mrs. Spalding was especially beset with these tales of horror.   "But," said the husband, with an honest pride, "it didn't move her a hair."

A Sunday on shore.—An incident, by the way, should be noted here.   The party took boat at Pittsburg.   Saturday night found them between Cairo and St. Louis.   Mrs. Spalding, who seems to have had a good share both of courage and the conscience of the company, insisted that they should be put on shore to spend Sunday.   The captain and the passengers laughed at her scruples.   But she said, "Out on the plains we shall be at the mercy of the Fur Company, and must go on; here we can stop."

"But no boat will ever call at such an out-of-the-way place as this to take you off."

"We'll take the chances of that.   Put us on shore."

The New England home missionary marked that day in white which brought such a rare accession to his little meeting in the schoolhouse.   He said it was like an angel's visit.   Early Monday morning a great puffing was heard below, and a grand steamer, better than the one they had left, rounded to at their signal and took them on board. Sixty miles above they overtook the other boat hopelessly stranded on a sand-bar.

At St. Louis the missionaries found the American Fur Company fitting out their annual expedition for the mountains.   But as the two wives were along, they could not have secured a place in the caravan had not Whitman been in special favor by his services rendered the year before.   It seems that, on his previous trip, a few days out from Council Bluffs, the cholera had broken out, and the demoralized men, dropping their packs, began to flee in a perfect rout.   But Dr. Whitman, who, added to his great strength, had skill and tact, was equal to the emergency.   Throwing off his coat, he sweated the patients over the boiling camp kettles, administered powerful remedies, and so stayed the pestilence and restored order.   The men were now as grateful as they had been before cool and contemptuous; and when an arrow's head had been extracted from behind the festering spine of a comrade, and his life saved, their admiration knew no bounds.

Having secured the company's pledge, they pressed on by boat to Liberty Landing. Here Spalding purchased mules, (wild he found them,) fifteen or twenty horses, as many cows, and two wagons, not forgetting a quart of seed wheat.   With this retinue he started for Council Bluffs, while Whitman waited, with the women and the goods, for the company's boat.   After some days that boat passed, purposely leaving them behind.   Through this bad faith, he was obliged to send forward to Spalding for horses, and to overtake him as he could by land.   This part of the trip was peculiarly trying. Spalding especially, who, for his wife's sake, was not yet altogether happy in going, seemed to be the sport of a very ill fortune.   But in the review even he could see a comic side to his mishaps.   A mule kicked him.   He was terribly shaken by the ague. In crossing a ferry an unruly cow, which he had laid hold of, jumped overboard, taking him along for ballast.   A tornado scattered his cattle, swept away his tent, tore his blankets from him while the ague turn was on, and left him to be drenched by the rain, with the usual consequences to one who takes calomel for his medicine.

It did not help the case any to learn, when they were within twenty-five miles of Council Bluffs, that the Fur Company's convoy had started, and were already five and a half days out on the plains.

"'Twas a poor chance," said the narrator, "for us greenhorns.   They were old trappers with fresh horses, while our teams were already jaded.   And I said—I was terribly sick, you know—'we can't overtake them; we shall have to go back.'   But my wife constantly affirmed, 'I have started for the Rocky Mountains, and I expect to go there!'"

And now commenced a series of marked interpositions.   It was pure faith and no sight at all to push on after that cavalcade.   The trappers evidently designed to keep ahead, and so induce the missionaries to turn back.   But to secure the protection of the convoy was indispensable, and God took care of His own.

"It was a desperate race," said the missionary, kindling at the remembrance, "but we won it.   They had to halt and fill up ravines and make roads, preparing the way of the Lord, you see.   This detained them four days.   Just where He stopped them the year before with the cholera, He stayed them again; not, as at the Red Sea, by taking off the wheels, but by setting the axles on fire.   In their haste to get away from us they had forgotten to take sufficient wheel-grease.   To burn wood for ashes, going ten miles out of their way to find it, and to kill two oxen for the fat necessary for this compound, took four days more.   And then, at Loup Fork, still four other days were lost in finding the ford and drying their goods, wet in crossing.   Meanwhile we were pressing on behind, and the Lord helped us.   The day before we reached Loup

Fork we rode from daylight—it was late in May—till two o'clock at night. One horse broke down and was turned loose, and my wife fainted by the way. A signal gun at the ford brought answer from the other side, and we camped. The convoy started early* in the morning, but left a man to show us across, and late that night we missionaries filed into their camp, and took the place reserved for us, two messes *west* of the captain's tent, and so we won the race by two lengths!"

Once among them, nothing could exceed the kindness of the men. "The choicest buffalo morsels were always kept for our ladies. But sick or well, we had to go on. We were two hundred souls and six hundred animals. Everything was in the strictest military order, for hostile Indians continually hovered on our flanks. At night we camped, with the animals solid in the center. The tents and wagons were disposed around them; and outside of all sentinels marched their steady round. Each day two hunters and two packers went out for buffalo. Each night, save when we had lost the way, they overtook us at the appointed camp with four mule-loads of meat. This was our only subsistence."

"Did they never fail to find game?"

"Yes, once or twice, and then we had to go hungry."

On the 6th of June we were at Fort Laramie. Wife was growing weaker and weaker.

"You must stay here," said the captain; "Mrs. Spalding will die for want of bread."

"No," said she, "I started to go over the mountains in the name of my Savior, and I must go on."

Independence Day at the 'Divide.'—July 4th, they entered the South Pass. Mrs. Spalding fainted that morning, and thought she was about to die. As they laid her upon the ground, she said: "Don't put me on that horse again. Leave me and save yourselves. Tell mother I am glad I came."

But the caravan stopped on the "Divide," and sent back for her, and she was borne on. She soon revived, and three hours afterward they saw the waters trickling toward the Pacific. And there—it was Independence Day, six years before Frémont, following in the footsteps of these women, gained the name of the "Path-finder,"—they, alighting from their horses and kneeling on the other half of the continent, with the Bible in one hand and the American flag in the other, took possession of it as the home of American mothers, and of the Church of Christ.

Just beyond was the great mountain rendezvous, the end of the convoy's route, a kind of neutral ground, where multitudes of Indians were gathered for trade. There were rough mountaineers there who had not seen a white woman since they had left the homes of their childhood. Some of them came to meet the missionaries, and wept as they took their wives by the hand. "From that day," said one of them, "I was a better man." But best of all, here met them a greeting party of the Nez Perces. They were the happiest men you ever saw. Their women took possession of Mrs. Spalding, and the gladness they showed, not less than the biscuit-root and the trout with which they fed her, revived her spirit. From that hour she began to mend; and from that hour her future and theirs were one.

Ten days of rest here, and the journey was resumed. The remainder of the way, if shorter, was no less perilous, and they had asked in dismay, "What shall we do for a convoy?" But God took care of them. He sent an English trading company to the rendezvous that year—an unusual thing—and with them they completed the trip.

It was the 29th of November when they reached the Columbia River. They had left civilization the 21st of May, a long journey, but not the trip of two summers to which they had made up their minds.

And now they were at home amid a nation that had no homes; they had found a resting place among restless wanderers. But faith had become sight; the first battle had been fought and won. White women had come safely over the mountains; cattle and horses had been kept secure from Indian raiders; a *wagon* had been brought through, "*the first wheel that had ever pressed the sage.*" Whitman had demonstrated to himself that an emigration could cross from Missouri to Oregon; and when, six years afterward, he led a company of a thousand along the same track, he demonstrated it to the world and saved Oregon, and with it California, to the United States.

The true Indian policy.—The old missionary's story is not half told, but we must cut it short. Whitman took the Cayuses at Waiilatpu (Wy-ee-lat-poo,) near Walla Walla; Spalding camped 120 miles farther up the Snake River, among the Nez Perces. He found a people without a hoe, or plow, or hoof of cattle; savages, who feasted when the hunt was good, but starved through the long winters. Eleven years afterward they were settled in homes; their crops of grain had reached from 20,000 to 30,000 bushels a year. The cows which the missionaries brought had multiplied for the Indians into numerous herds; gardens and orchards were planted; the sheep which the English residents denied them, but which the Sandwich Islanders gave, had grown to flocks. In the school which Mrs. Spalding taught, carrying a young child in her arms, were 500 pupils. A church of a hundred members had been gathered. The tongue of the people, hitherto without a character, had been reduced to writing. A patriarchal government, with a code of laws, had been established; the Sabbath was

observed. Upon the first printing press west of the mountains, and *that* presented to
the mission by the native church at Honolulu—the typesetting, press work, and binding done by the missionary's own hand—were printed a few school-books, the native
code of laws, a small collection of hymns, and the Gospel of Matthew.

St. Bartholomew's Day in Oregon.—And then came that tornado of rapine and murder
at Waiilatpu, evoked, there is abundant evidence to believe, by the Jesuit Fathers.
Whitman, with fourteen others, was massacred. The killing lasted through eight
days, and, in the midst of it, the Catholic priests baptized Indian children whose
hands were stained with the victim's blood.

A young woman, already outraged in the presence of her dying brother, who had
gone to the Father's house for safety, was thrust out each night for twenty days to the
hated embrace of an Indian chief. He called it making her his wife, but she plead that
she might be killed. Spalding, visiting Whitman at the time, fled for his life to his
faithful Nez Perces. Six days he was without food, feeling his way, sore-footed, by
night, and hiding when the dawn appeared. There was a hasty gathering of the
household, a journey of two hundred miles to the settlements, in mid-winter, and the
mission came to an end. Almost blind himself, and broken in constitution, he watched
for many months by the bedside of his wife, dying from that exposure; watched till
she passed through the river to the Celestial Mountains and the land beyond.

Upon the records of Congress, printed through what intrigue and connivance let him
tell who can, stands a paper known as "Ex. Doc. No. 38, 35th Congress, 1st session."
It claims to be—it *is* a statement full of perjuries and perversions—"A History of Protestantism in Oregon, by the Rev. J. B. A. Brouillet, vicar-general of Walla Walla."
Further on it calls itself an "Account of the murder of Dr. Whitman, and the ungrate-
ful calumnies of H. H. Spalding, Protestant missionary." The Nez Perces mission-
grounds, abandoned (so say the officials) by the American board, are in litigation to-
day for recovery, and the Jesuits are thrusting themselves upon that very tribe redeemed from heathenism through the labors of this same Protestant missionary. Who
shall now say we have a State without a church? O, ye priests and politicians, for
this wrong unparalleled, you shall yet stand condemned at the bar of an outraged public sentiment; and, after that, at the bar of God! "How long, O Lord, how long!"

From Elijah White, Esq., United States Indian agent, 1843.

APRIL 1, 1843.

*   *   *   Left the following day for the station of Mr. Spalding,
among the Nez Perces, 120 miles over a most verdant and delightful grazing district,
well watered but badly timbered.   *   *   *   The chiefs met us with civility,
gravity, and dignified reserve, but the missionaries with joyful countenances and glad
hearts.   *   *   *   Spent a season in the school, hearing them read, sing, and spell;
at the same time examined their printing (with the pen) and writing, and can hardly
avoid here saying I was happily surprised and greatly interested at seeing such numbers so far advanced and so eagerly pursuing after knowledge. The next day (December 4, 1842) I visited their plantations, rude, to be sure, but successfully carried on, so
far as raising the necessaries of life were concerned; and it was most gratifying to witness their fondness and care for their little herds, pigs, poultry, &c.   *   *   *
I was ushered into the presence of the assembled chiefs to the number of twenty-two,
and a large number of the common people.   *   *   *   The gravity, fixed attention, and decorum of these sons of the forest was calculated to make for them a most
favorable impression.   *   *   *   I gave them to understand how highly Mr. and
Mrs. Spalding were prized by the numerous whites, and with what pleasure the great
chief had given them a paper to encourage them to come here to teach them what they
were now so diligently employed in obtaining, in order that they and their children
might become good, wise, and happy.   *   *   *   Mr. McKinley, of Fort Walla
Walla, spoke concisely of his long residence among them as their trader, and forcibly
of their (to him) unexpected advancement in the arts and sciences.

Next arose Mr. McKay: "I appear as one from the long sleep of death. You know of
the death of my father on board the ship Tonquin; I was but a youth. I have mingled
with you in bloody wars and profound peace; I have stood in your midst surrounded
with plenty, and suffered with you in seasons of scarcity. We have had our days of
wild sport and nights of watching, till I vanished from among men, left the Hudson's
Bay Company, and retired to my plantation; was silent as one dead; the voice of my
brother aroused me; I mounted horse; am here; I am glad it is so. I came at the call of
the great chief, whose children are more numerous than the stars in the heavens or the
leaves in the forest. Will you hear and be advised? You will. Your wonderful improvements in the arts and sciences prove you are no fools; surely you will hear."

Chiefs speak; Five Crows, (Pahet-ko-ko,) about 45, neatly attired in English cos-
tume, wealthy, and owns some 2,000 horses, stepped gravely but modestly to the table:
"I am but a youth, but my feelings urge me to speak. I have listened to what has
been said. I have great hopes that brighter days are before us; have been groping
for something, hardly knew what, as in darkness; here it is."

The bloody chief (Noo-son-ki-oon,) not less than 90 years: "I speak to-day; to-morrow perhaps I die. I am the oldest chief of the tribe; was the great chief when your brothers Lewis and Clark visited this country; they honored me with their friendship and counsel. I showed them my numerous wounds received in bloody battle with the Snakes; they told me it was not good; it was better to be at peace; gave me a flag of peace; I held it up high; we met, we talked, but never fought again. Clark pointed to this day; we have long waited; sent three of our sons to the rising sun to obtain the Book from Heaven; two of them sleep with their fathers. I am glad to live to see this day; shall soon be still and quiet in death."

Other chiefs spoke.

Ellis was appointed high chief; a sensible man of 32, reading, speaking, and writing the English language tolerably well; has a fine small plantation, few sheep, some neat cattle, and no less than 1,100 head of horses. Then came the feast; our ox was fat, and cooked and served up in a manner reminding me of the days of yore. We ate beef, corn, and peas to our fill, and in good cheer took the pipe; when Rev. Mr. Spalding, Messrs. McKinley, Rogers, and McKay wished from our boatmen a song; it was no sooner given than returned by the Indians, and repeated again and again in high cheer. I thought it a good time, and requested all having any claim or grievance against Mr. Spalding to meet me and the high chief at evening in the council room, and requested Mr. Spalding to do the same. We met at six and ended at eleven, having accomplished much business in the happiest manner.

The next day we had our last meeting. I made them, in the name of our great chief, a present of 50 hoes, (heavy,) to be distributed by Mr. Spalding among their industrious poor. I then turned, and, with good effect, desired all the chiefs to look upon the congregation as their own children, and then pointed to Mr. Spalding and lady, and told the chiefs and all present to look upon them as their father and mother, and to treat them in all respects as such. Thus closed this mutually happy and interesting meeting, and mounting our horses for home, Mr. and Mrs. Spalding and the chiefs accompanied us four or five miles, when we took leave of them in the pleasantest manner, not a single circumstance having occurred to mar our peace, or shake each other's confidence.

After a severe journey of four days, reached Waiilatpu, Dr. Whitman's station, where we had many most unpleasant matters to settle. Feather Cap commenced weeping. Tauwat-wai said the whites were much more to blame than the Indians; that three-fourths of them, though they taught the purest doctrines, practiced the greatest abominations, referring to the base conduct of many in the Rocky Mountains; acknowledged it as his opinion that the mill was burnt purposely by some disaffected persons toward Dr. Whitman. The mill, lumber, and great quantity of grain was burnt by Catholic Indians, instigated by Romanists, to break up the Protestant mission, and prevent supplies to the on-coming emigration by Dr. Whitman. * * And here allow me to say, except at Wascopum, the missionaries of the upper country are too few in number, * * and in too defenseless state for their own safety. * * Rev. Mr. and Mrs. Spalding, whose zeal and untiring industry for the benefit of the people of their charge entitles them to our best consideration, have a school of some two hundred and twenty-four, in constant attendance, most successfully carried forward, which promises to be of great usefulness to both sexes and all ages.

ELIJAH WHITE,
Sub-Agent of Indian Affairs West of the Rocky Mountains.

T. Hartley Crawford, Esq.,
Commissioner Indian Affairs, Washington, D. C.

Department of War, Office of Indian Affairs,
November 25, 1844.

Communications have been received from Dr. Elijah White, sub-Indian agent for the Indians in Oregon Territory. * * They contain much of interest in considerable detail. The establishment of white settlements from the United States in that remote region seems to be attended with the circumstances that have always arisen out of the conversion of an American wilderness into a cultivated and improved region, modified by the great advance of the present time in morals, and benevolent and religious institutions. It is very remarkable that there should be so soon several well-supported, well-attended, and well-conducted schools in Oregon. The Nez Perces tribe of Indians have adopted a few simple and plain laws as their code, which will teach them self-restraint, and is the beginning of government on their part.

Respectfully submitted.

T. HARTLEY CRAWFORD.

Hon. William Wilkins,
Secretary of War.

From Elwood Evans.

Again, the Hudson's Bay Company professed neutrality. See Governor Ogden's speech to the Indians when he went to redeem the captives. See, too, what he says when he tells the Indians that they thought such acts would prove acceptable to the company. The logic of the latter proves the outbreak to have been liable to follow the too-literal appreciation of the education of the Indian mind as to their hatred of the Boston; and neutrality in such a case is but sympathy with the wrong-doer. And history, therefore, must accept the inexorable logic that though Dr. Whitman had committed no such acts as seemed in the eyes of the company to justify such retaliation, yet some events it was a character of service which might have been expected from their alliance with the company.

Again, the company's servants could travel in the hostile country in perfect safety. Any Catholic could enjoy similar immunity—*a priori* the Indians were hostile, not to whites, but to American Protestants.

Again, there is no doubt but that either the Hudson's Bay Company or the Catholic missionaries could have prevented any outbreak of hostility on the part of Indians. They failed to exercise such influence. They omitted to do a Christian, humane duty. Such an omission is as criminal, morally, as direct commission of acts inciting to hostility.

History, therefore, to do justice, will condemn the criminal teaching of a creature, hardly accountable, to hate a class. It will palliate the Indian who could not discriminate between "no intercourse" and open hostility. It will blame those who, provoking a storm, were not gifted with the power to control the elements, even had they the desire to do so. Nor will it excuse them because by a proffer of sympathy to stay the sacrifice of life they endeavored to relieve the captives. That Governor Ogden could relieve those captives, that the Roman clergy could stay in the midst of the hostile Indians, proves too much. The same influence, had it been properly exerted, would have avoided the massacre. But we must go deeper for the cause of the massacre. The history of the agency of Protestant missions in encouraging American settlement; the advent of settlers; the uniform first visit to the Whitman station; the treaty of 1846, which decided that the days of the occupancy by the company of the Territory were numbered, and that they had been baffled in getting Columbia River for the line, explain the causes of chagrin of the company. The policy of the company, pursued everywhere, of making the Indian subservient in time of peace, auxiliary in event of war, finishes the matter. There is no necessity to charge that the Indians who killed the inmates of Waiilatpu, on the specified occasion, were directly incited to that act. There was no time, from 1836 down to November, 1847, when such advice was necessary.—*Elwood Evans's History, chap.* 19.

How naturally the query arises, "Why is the Catholic exempt from danger; why can the Hudson's Bay Company employé remain amid these scenes of blood and Indian vengeance against the white race, at peace, undisturbed, and what is more loathsome, neutral in such a conflict; why can the priest administer the rites of his church to those Indians who are making war against Christians—even flocking to him—when you and other missionaries are fleeing for your lives because you are a missionary and an American?" Think you the conviction will not follow that the uncivilized Indian was, at best, supposing that these bloody deeds were acceptable service to those whom he continued to regard as patrons and friends? Let your narrative really illustrate that "inasmuch as they did these things unto me" because I was an American and a Protestant, that any and all Americans at that time would have suffered like consequences, then will flow the corollary—distilled truth, the logic of history—Catholics and Britons were exempt. The American missionaries were the apostles paving the way for American occupancy—the avant couriers of Oregon-Americanization. The Hudson's Bay Company—with its auxiliaries, the Catholic missionaries—were making their last grand struggle for the sole and unlimited control of the Indian mind. They expected they were carrying out the wishes of their teachers. See Ogden's speech to the Indians, where he boldly and openly owns that "the Indians believed they would receive the approbation of the company."—*Honorable Elwood Evans's Letter to Rev. H. H. Spaulding, Olympia, June* 30, 1868.

That record (history) is the best monument to the faithful who died at their posts—words of tribute or panegyric from any pen sink into insignificance when compared to American blood crying aloud from unmade graves at Waiilatpu. "Remember this, we suffered because we were Americans!" That mound called Whitman's grave, speaks louder "the deep damnation of his taking off" than could most eloquent tribute inscribed upon the granite shaft, lifting its towering head to heaven itself; for it calls to mind that none were spared of American blood to do the last sad rites to these martyrs.

Nor need you fear that the missionary heroines, who proved that woman could go to Oregon, and live and die there, will ever be forgotten. When this generation shall have passed away, when envious neighbors, vieing with each other who did most to bring American institutions to the shores of the Pacific, shall lie motionless in death, and thousands now unborn shall travel by rail over that then untraveled route, that little missionary caravan will come back to memory, to last as long as the eternal mountains. That transit, now stripped of all terrors, difficulty and danger will be recognized as the direct consequence of that heroic journey, showing what woman could do. Nor will it be forgotten that Oregon was then deemed worthless because of its remoteness and supposed inaccessibility. Those women dispelled both these false theories; demonstrated that Oregon could be peopled from the United States; showed its continuity to the Pacific shore, joint occupancy or non-occupancy, call it what you please, was superseded by American *sole* occupancy. Oregon was saved by reason of those women, engaged in a soul-saving mission, west of the Rocky Mountains.—*Hon. Elwood Evans's Letter to Rev. H. H. Spalding, Olympia, W. T., June 30, 1868.*

Report of the United States Indian Agent for 1843.

WILLAMETTE VALLEY, OREGON, *November* 15, 1843.

HONORED SIR: Since my arrival I have had the honor of addressing you some three or four communications, the last conveyed by the Hudson's Bay Company's express over the Rocky Mountains via Canada. The day following we left those Walla-Wallas and Cayuses, to pay a visit to the Nez Perces. In two days we were at Mr. Spalding's station. The Nez Perces came together in greater numbers than on any former occasion for years, and all the circumstances combining to favor it, received us most cordially. Their improvemet during the winter, in reading, singing, writing, weaving, &c., was considerable, and the enlargement of their plantations, with the increased variety and quantities of the various kinds of grains and products, now vigorously shooting forth, connected with the better state of cultivation, and their universally good fences, were certainly most encouraging.

Spending three days with this interesting tribe and their missionaries in the pleasantest manner, they accepted my invitation to visit with me the Cayuses and Walla-Wallas, and assist, by their influence, to bring them into the same regulations.

Mr. Spalding and Ellis, the high chief, and every other chief and brave of importance, and some five hundred of the men and women accompanied us to Waiilatpu, a distance of one hundred and thirty miles, where we met the Cayuses and Walla-Wallas in a mass, and spent some six days in adjusting principles, so as to receive the Cayuses into civil compact, which done, and a chief elected, much to the satisfaction of both whites and Indians, I ordered two fat oxen killed, and wheat, salt, &c., to be distributed.

The last year's report, in which was incorporated Mr. Lewis's Oregon speech and Captain Spalding's statements of hundreds of unoffending Indians being shot down annually by men under his (Dr. McLaughlin's) control, afflicts the gentlemen of the Hudson's Bay Company, and is utterly without foundation.

Respectfully, yours,

ELIJAH WHITE,
Sub-agent of Indian Affairs West of the Rocky Mounta ns.

Hon. J. M. PORTER,
Secretary of War, Washington, D. C.

DEPARTMENT OF WAR, OFFICE OF INDIAN AFFAIRS,
Washington, D. C., November 24, 1845.

Two interesting and very instructive reports have been received from the sub-agent west of the Rocky Mountains. They present that country in a new and important light to the consideration of the public. The advancement in civilization by the numerous tribes in that remote and hitherto neglected portion of our territory, with so few advantages, is a matter of surprise. Indeed, the red men of that region would almost seem to be of a different order from those with whom we have been in more familiar intercourse. A few years since the face of a white man was almost unknown to them. Now, through the benevolent policy of the various Christian churches and the indefatigable exertions of the missionaries in their employ, they have prescribed and well adapted rules for their government, which are observed and respected to a degree worthy the most intelligent whites.

Numerous schools have grown up in their midst, at which their children are acquiring the most important and useful information. They have already advanced (especially the Nez Perces Nation) to a degree of civilization that promises the most beneficial results to them and their brethren on this side of the mountains, with whom they may, and no doubt will, at no distant day be brought into intercourse. They are turning their attention to agricultural pursuits, and, with but few of the necessary utensils in their possession, already produce sufficient, in some instances, to meet their every want.

Among some of the tribes hunting has been almost entirely abandoned, many individuals looking wholly to the soil for support. The lands are represented as extremely fertile and the climate healthy, agreeable, and uniform.

Under these circumstances, so promising in their consequences and so grateful to the feelings of the philanthropist, it would seem to be the duty of the Government of the United States to encourage their advancement and still further aid their progress in the path of civilization.

    Respectfully submitted,

W. MEDILL.

Hon. WM. L. MARCY,
    Secretary of War.

Testimony of General Alvord, of the United States Army.

He (Colonel Steptoe) often descanted on the manly traits and Christian perseverance and fortitude of Timothy, (a Nez Perces chief,) and many of the Nez Perces. Accounts concur as to the remarkable preservation by the Nez Perces of the habits derived from the missionaries a dozen years ago. Such docility deserves encouragement. Their devotion to our people, our arms, and our Government, has also endeared them to all who have been watching the history of their position.—*General Alvord's letter to G. H. Atkinson, D. D., of Portland, dated Fort Vancouver, December* 28, 1858.

I concur cordially in the above.

GEO. ABERNATHY.

I concur in the sentiments of General Alvord.

JOEL PALMER.

Question. Can you concur in the sentiments contained in the printed memorial herewith sent? Please sign and return.

I heartily concur.

GEO. ABERNATHY.

I concur with all my heart.

J. S. GRIFFIN.
WM. GEIGER.
A. HINMAN.
J. N. GILBERT.

We cheerfully concur.

GUSTAVUS HINES.
W. C. HATCH.
O. DICKINSON.
A. Z. WALLAR.
JOEL PALMER.

ALBANY, OREGON, *October* 22, 1868.

To his excellency Governor Ballard, of the Territory of Idaho, ex-officio superintendent of Indian Affairs:

The undersigned, a committee appointed by the presbytery of Oregon, (Old School,) to devise measures for the renewal of the work of Christian missions among the nation of the Nez Perces Indians, and to promote the reinstatement of our respected ministerial brother, the Rev. H. H. Spalding, in that field of his early and successful labors, would respectfully and earnestly request your excellency to appoint Mr. Spalding superintendent of instruction, under the treaty of 1856, and would respectfully submit the following considerations therefor:

1st. Our long personal acquaintance with Mr. Spalding and knowledge of his early successful labors in that field impel us to regard him as eminently qualified for the position.

2d. His familiar acquaintance with the native language, reduced by him to a written state, several school books being prepared and portions of Scripture translated by him, and printed on the first press on this coast, the only instance of the kind, it is belived, among the Indian tribes on these Pacific shores. These books are held at this time above all price by the Nez Perces.

3d. His great, perhaps unparalleled success as a missionary in Christianizing and introducing the usages of civilization among that people during the eleven years spent among them, and until driven away in the year 1847, as attested by the superior intelligence, enterprise, and good order still characterizing and distinguishing them from the surrounding tribes. To this hundreds of our citizens, civil and military officers, miners, travelers, and others of most reliable character, bear a uniform testimony. Among these we would name Commodore Wilkes, an eye-witness in 1841, Rev. Gustavus Hines, in 1843, General Joel Palmer, in 1846, Colonel Steptoe, Agent Anderson, and Governor Daniels. The country, on the arrival of Mr. Spalding, in 1836, was emphatically a wilderness; uncultivated; not a hoe, plow, or hoof of cattle; the savages starving on their meagre supply of roots and fishes; ignorant of letters, of agriculture, of the Sabbath, and of human salvation.

4th. That this scene should so soon be changed, the "desert to bud and blossom," the fields to wave with grain, 15,000 to 20,000 bushels of grain harvested yearly by the Indians, orchards and gardens planted, cattle roving in bands, schools established, in which from 100 to 500 souls were in daily attendance, women spinning, over 100 professors adorning the Christian faith, a church organized and family altars erected, speak volumes for the fidelity and efficiency of Mr. Spalding and his estimable wife.

5th. The strong alliance and unwavering friendship of the Nez Perces to the Americans, while all the surrounding tribes have been at times hostile and repeatedly in arms against the United States, their friendship being fairly and clearly attributable to the instruction and influence of Mr. Spalding, render him worthy of the most favorable consideration of the Government.

6th. The personal hazards, sacrifices, and perils of Mr. Spalding and wife, and Dr. Whitman and wife (the first white women to hazard the Rocky Mountains and the route across the continent), in opening the great emigrant route in 1836, thus securing the settling of this coast by Americans, their constant aid and friendship to the wayworn emigrant, their watchful and untiring labors in defeating the intrigues of English diplomacy, and securing this vast Pacific West to our country, should secure to them a gratitude and esteem not to be forgotten.

7th. The oft-expressed and strong desire of the Nez Perces for Mr. Spalding's return, and his constant and full reciprocation of that desire to live among them and devote his life to their spiritual good and social elevation, is all a consideration not to be lightly regarded.

8th. No other man lives capable of translating the Scriptures into their language, and of preaching to them the Gospel so intelligently as Mr. Spalding.

9th. The honor of the United States is involved in the faithful execution of the treaty of 1856 for the purchase of that country, which could not have been successfully negotiated without the liberal provisions for schools and teachers which it contains; the disregard of which hitherto subjects our Government to the charge of bad faith and a failure to appreciate the fidelity of a people whose integrity and friendship have often saved our frontiers from the blood and desolation of savage war, and the National Treasury the expense of millions of dollars in military expenditures.

Agent Anderson, for several years in charge of the Nez Perces, does not, in our judgment, exaggerate in saying that the "friendly relations always maintained by the Nez Perces with the Americans is in a great measure to be attributed to the influence and teachings of Mr. Spalding," and that, in his "opinion, Mr. S., by his own personal labors, has accomplished more good to this tribe than all the money expended by the Government has been able to effect." All of which is respectfully submitted.

With high personal esteem we are, sir, your obedient servants,

EDWARD R. GEARY,
Former Superintendent of that Territory.
WM. J. MONTEITH,
D. B. RICE,
Committee of Presbytery.

To his excellency Governor Ballard, of the Territory of Idaho:

The following is respectfully submitted:

We, a committee appointed in May, 1868, by the Oregon Presbytery of the United Presbyterian Church, to investigate the case of the Rev. H. H. Spalding, in his relations as missionary to the Nez Perces tribe of Indians, did report to the above-named presbytery, which report was unanimously accepted by that body, and the substance of which is embodied in the above memorial, as prepared by a committee representing the presbytery of the Old School Church in Oregon, and addressed to his excellency, Ballard, governor of Idaho.

We, therefore, heartily concur in and subscribe to the above memorial, earnestly requesting his excellency to act on it as soon as practicable.

T. S. KENDALL,
JOHN McCOY,
Committee of Presbytery of U. P. Church.

We, ministers, elders, and members of the above-named O. S. and U. P. Churches of Oregon, and acquaintances of Rev. H. H. Spalding, from personal knowledge or testimony, concur in the statements made in the above memorial.

[Here follows a list of five or six hundred names, numbering among them some of the very best men in the State.]

We, citizens of Oregon, and old acquaintances of Rev. H. H. Spalding, heartily concur in the statements contained in the above memorial.

JOHN CONNOR, *Merchant.*
L. F. GROVER, *Ex-Congressman.*
EDWARD FREELAND, *Postmaster.*
GRANVILL BABAR, *Judge.*
S. A. JOHNS, *Judge.*
R. H. DUNCAN.
A. HOLT.
S. E. HOLT.
And perhaps a thousand others.

Testimony from Washington Territory to loyalty of Nez Perces Indians, and to Whitman and Spalding.

SEATTLE, WASHINGTON TERRITORY, *March* 24, 1869.

JAMES BLAKELEY, *and others, committee to examine executive document* 38:

GENTLEMEN: In reply to your circular of 4th instant, we would say that we cheerfully concur in the sentiments set forth in the printed memorial accompanying it; and further, from reliable information, and in part from our own knowledge, we accord with the statements contained in the letter of J. W. Anderson, esq., former Indian agent in charge of the Nez Perces nation, as to the influence of the Rev. H. H. Spalding over said tribe.

We also answer that it is our belief that it was by the labors and self-denials of the Protestant missionaries, and their heroic wives, at an early day in Oregon—through the information given by them, both to the people and the Government of the United States—that this whole region was secured. We further believe it to be true that it was through their efforts that the country was thrown open to and settled by the people of the United States; and that in an especial degree are we indebted to the lamented Whitman, whose presence at the city of Washington, in March, 1843, very opportunely prevented the consummation of a transfer of Oregon to England.

GEO. F. WHITWORTH,
Chief Clerk Indian Department, including Nez Perces Nation, and Minister Reunited Presbyterian Church.
D. BAGLEY,
Presiding Elder Protestant Methodist Church.
J. D. DRIVER,
M. E. Church, Agent American Bible Society.
G. H. GREER.
C. H. HALE,
Former Superintendent Indian Affairs, including Nez Perces Nation.
C. T. HUNTINGTON,
Chief Clerk Indian Department, W. T.

From Governor Evans, Chief Justice Hewet, &c.

OLYMPIA, *March* 26, 1869.

We, the undersigned citizens of Washington Territory, have read the foregoing memorial praying the appointment of the Rev. H. H. Spalding as superintendent of instruction for the Nez Perces tribe of Indians, and cordially concur in said prayer, as also in the reasons for said action as set forth in said memorial.

S. D. HOWE,
Assessor Internal Revenue and former Commissioner Nez Perces treaty, 1863.
S. GARFIELDE,
Surveyor-General W. T., Delegate to Congress.
A. G. COOK,
Attorney at Law.
T. W. REED,
Former Speaker of Legislative Assembly, W. T. and I. T.
C. C. HEWET,
Chief Justice Washington Territory.
B. T. YANTIS.
T. F. McELROY.
H. K. HINES,
Presiding Elder Methodist Episcopal Church.
ELWOOD EVANS,
Late Secretary W. T., including Nez Perces Nation.
E. S. SMITH,
Secretary Washington Territory.

The Methodist Episcopal Church, the Baptist, the Christian, the Congregational, the Presbyterian Church, the United Presbyterian Church, and reunited churches, in their ecclesiastical bodies, have concurred in said memorial.

What two missionary women have done for the country—Hon. Elwood Evans—Success of missions the wealth of the nation.

After the discovery of America by Columbus, it was not long before the Atlantic Ocean had ceased to be regarded as a great barrier to an advent to the Atlantic shores of the American continent. Indeed, long before the first settlement of New England the continent itself was the obstacle to westward progress, then already the path to empire. To cross this immensity of land, or to avoid it being crossed, really had become the problem before the pilgrim fathers thought of settlement in America. The latter theory was regarded the one which needed solution. None were bold enough to attempt crossing the continent itself, yet this was the task the Oregon emigrant had to accomplish or to make the voyage around Cape Horn. The history of the Oregon controversy develops the fact that it long continued to be doubted whether it were possible to people Oregon overland from the United States, or whether that Territory must receive its population by sea, via Cape Horn. If the former failed, then Great Britain, with her over-glutted centers of population, could use Oregon as an escape-valve, and all the probabilities seemed to indicate that British colonization would ultimately settle the Oregon controversy by maturing occupancy and possession.

But a third of a century ago two heroic, self-sacrificing American women found the solution of this problem of doubt and uncertainty. Actuated by as holy an impulse as inspired the Puritan fathers to spread the blessings of the Christian religion in new lands, they undertook the pilgrimage to Oregon to convert the Indians. What sermon could be more eloquent than that silent readiness to undertake such a journey? No heroism more sublime than their willingness to go. How sanctified has been that preaching! How shortly after the fruit appeared, in opening to Americanization the vast region west of the Rocky Mountains preparing it for the homes of men, women, and children. If women could reach Oregon overland the settlement of territorial claim was attained. That interesting incident of the past was the sure harbinger of what we are now about realizing. The great engineering and utilitarian idea of the 19th century is about to be consummated. The continent is crossed by a railroad. After American women had traversed the broad plains and crossed the great mountain chains of the American continent, it was needless further to search for a "Strait of Anian." That journey, accomplished safely, preceded the emigrant wagon road. As a natural consequence the railway has been substituted, the commerce of the Pacific and the eastern seas is concentrated in American cities on the Pacific shores, and the United States of America is the leading power of the world.

The example of the sainted heroines—one of whom (Mrs. Dr. Marcus Whitman) was slain at her post of duty by the perfidious savage for whose benefit she had gone into exile from home, kindred, and all its endearments, and the other (Mrs. Rev. H. H. Spalding) lies under the clod in an Oregon valley—was soon followed by a hardy band of men, women, and children. In each of these was a living argument of the integrity of claim of their nation to this territory. They were alike devoted to the glorious task of dedicating the wilderness to become a home for God's creatures, and reclaiming for their country a vast expanse of valuable territory, well-nigh lost by the "masterly inactivity" and apathy of the Government.—*Hon. Elwood Evans's (late secretary Washington Territory) address at Port Townsend, W. T., January,* 1869.

THE MARTYR WHITMAN'S SERVICES TO THE EMIGRANT ROUTE.

HIS TERRIFIC WINTER JOURNEY THROUGH THE ROCKY MOUNTAINS—HIS SUCCESSFUL MISSION AT WASHINGTON.

However the political question between England and the United States as to the ownership of Oregon may be decided, Oregon will never be colonized overland from the United States. The world must assume a new face before the American wagons will make plain the road to the Columbia as they have to the Ohio.—*Edinburgh Review,* 1843.

SENATOR LANE OF OREGON ON THE MISSIONARY WHITMAN.

Among those who thus labored faithfully and unremittingly and with a singleness of purpose and self-sacrificing zeal which commanded the admiration and respect of all who observed his elevated and untiring labors, was the Rev. Marcus Whitman. Never, in my opinion, did missionary go forth to the field of his labors animated by a nobler purpose, or devote himself to his task with more earnestness and sincerity than this meek and Christian man. He arrived in 1836, and established his mission in the Waiilatpu country, east of the Cascade Mountains, and devoted his entire time to the education and improvement of the Indians, teaching them the arts of civilization, the mode of cultivating the soil, to plant, to sow, to reap, to do all the duties that pertain to civilized man. He erected mills, plowed their ground, sowed their crops, and assisted in gathering in their harvest.

About the time he had succeeded in teaching them some of these arts and the means of using some of these advantages, they rose against him without cause and without notice, and massacred him and his wife and many others who were at the mission at the time.—*General Lane in the House of Representatives, April,* 1856.

This vastly important emigrant route, thus established by the personal sacrifices and hazards of those two devoted missionaries, was saved to our country, as it was about to be extinguished by the false representations and wiles of the Hudson's Bay Company, by the personal hazards and hardships of that devoted missionary, Dr. Whitman, in the California mountains, in the winter of 1842 and 1843.

Those two missionary heroines, with Dr. Whitman, Dr. Gray, and myself, crossed the mountains in 1836, bringing the first cattle and wagons. In 1838 four lady missionaries—Mrs. Smith, Eells, and Walker, from New England, and Mrs. Gray, from New York—and their husbands, and Mr. Rogers, from Cincinnati, crossed, bringing cattle, but no wagons. Two lady missionaries crossed in 1839—Mrs. Griffin and Mrs. Miuger, from New York, and their husbands. In 1840 three missionary ladies from New York, Mrs. Smith, Clark, and Littlejohn, and their husbands, and the first emigrant lady, Mrs. Walker, and her husband, crossed the mountains and brought their wagons; but on reaching Fort Hall they were compelled to abandon their wagons by the representations of the Hudson's Bay Company, who declared that wagons never had passed and could not pass through the Snake country and the Blue Mountains to the Columbia. This Mrs. Walker and her husband went from Oregon to California in 1841—the first American lady in California.

In 1841 no missionaries crossed, but several emigrant families, bringing wagons, which, on reaching Fort Hall, suffered the same fate with those of 1840. In 1842 considerable emigration moved forward with ox teams and wagons, but on reaching Fort Hall the same story was told them and the teams were sacrificed, and the emigrant families reached Dr. Whitman's station late in the fall, in very destitute circumstances. About this time, as events proved, that shrewd English diplomatist, Governor Simpson, long a resident on the Northwest coast, reached Washington, after having arranged that an English colony of some 150 souls should leave the Selkirk Settlement on the Red River of the lakes in the spring of 1842, and cross the Rocky Mountains by the Saskatchawan Pass.

DR. WHITMAN'S WINTER JOURNEY, 1843.

The peculiar event that aroused Dr. Whitman and sent him through the mountains of New Mexico, during that terrible winter of 1843, to Washington, just in time to save this now so valuable country from being traded off by Webster to the shrewd Englishman for a "cod fishery" down east, was as follows: In October of 1842 our mission was called together, on business, at Waiilatpu—Dr. Whitman's station—and while in session, Dr. W. was called to Fort Walla-Walla to visit a sick man. While there the "brigade" for New Caledonia, fifteen bateaux, arrived at that point on their way up the Columbia, with Indian goods for the New Caledonia or Frazer River country. They were accompanied by some twenty chief factors, traders, and clerks of the Hudson's Bay Company, and Bishop Demois, who had crossed the mountains from Canada, in 1839—the first Catholic priest on this coast; Bishop Blanchett came at the same time.

While this great company were at dinner, an express arrived from Fort Colville, announcing the (to them) glad news that the colony from Red River had passed the Rocky Mountains and were near Colville. An exclamation of joy burst from the whole table, at first unaccountable to Doctor Whitman, till a young priest, perhaps not so discreet as the older, and not thinking that there was an American at the table, sprang to his feet, and swinging his hand, exclaimed: "Hurrah for Columbia! (Oregon.) America is too late; we have got the country." In an instant, as by instinct, Dr. Whitman saw through the whole plan, clear to Washington, Fort Hall, and all. He immediately arose from the table and asked to be excused, sprang upon his horse, and in a very short time stood with his noble "Cayuse," white with foam, before his door; and without stopping to dismount, he replied to our anxious inquiries with great decision and earnestness: "I am going to cross the Rocky Mountains and reach Washington this winter, God carrying me through, and bring out an emigration over the mountains next season, or this country is lost." The events soon developed that if that whole-souled American missionary was not the "son of a prophet," he guessed right when he said a "deep-laid scheme was about culminating which would deprive the United States of this Oregon, and it must be broken at once, or the country is lost." We united our remonstrances with those of sister Whitman, who was in deep agony at the idea of her husband perishing in the snows of the Rocky Mountains. We told him it would be a miracle if he escaped death either from starving, or freezing, or the savages, or the perishing of his horses, during the five months that would be required to make the only possible circuitous route, via Fort Hall, Toas, Santa Fé, and Bent Fort. His reply was that of my angel wife six years before: "I am ready not to be bound only, but to die at Jerusalem or in the snows of the Rocky Mountains for the name of the Lord Jesus or my country. I am a missionary, it is true, but my country needs me now." And taking leave of his missionary associates, his comfortable home, and his weeping companion, with but little hope of seeing them again in this world, he entered upon his fearful journey the 2d of October, 1842, and reached the city of Washington the 2d of March, 1843, with his face, nose, ears, hands, feet, and legs badly frozen. It is well that the good man did not live to see himself and his faithful associates robbed and their character slandered by that very Government he was ready to lay down his life for. It would have been to him, as it is to me, the most mournful event of my life.

Nothing but the continued outstretched hand of God, and his clothing of buffalo hides, with the fur inside, and his unyielding spirit, saved him from perishing from the intense cold.

On that terrible 13th of January, 1843, when so many in all parts of our country froze to death, the doctor, against the advice of his Mexican guide, left his camp in a deep gorge of the mountains of New Mexico, in the morning, to pursue his journey. But on reaching the divide, the cold became so intense, and the animals actually becoming maddened by the driving snows, the doctor saw his peril, and attempted to retrace his steps, and, if possible, to find his camp, as the only hope of saving their lives. But the drifting snow had totally obliterated every trace, and the air becoming almost as dark as night by the maddening storm, the doctor saw that it would be impossible for any human being to find camp, and commending himself and distant wife to his covenant-keeping God, he gave himself, his faithful guide, and animals up to their snowy grave, which was fast closing about them, when the guide, observing the ears of one of the mules intently bent forward, sprang upon him, giving him the reins, exclaiming: "This mule will find the camp if he can live to reach it." The doctor mounted another and followed. The faithful animal kept down the divide a short distance, and then turned square down the steep mountain. Through deep snow-drifts, over frightful precipices, down, down, he pushed, unguided and unurged, as if he knew the lives of the two men and the fate of the great expedition depended upon his endurance and his faithfulness, and into the thick timber, and stopped suddenly over a bare spot, and as the doctor dismounted—the Mexican was too far gone— behold the very fire-place of their morning camp! Two brands of fire were yet alive and smoking; plenty of timber in reach. The buffalo hides had done much to protect the doctor, and providentially he could move about and collect dry limbs, and soon had a rousing fire. The guide revived, but both were badly frozen. They remained in this secluded *hole* in the mountains several days, till the cold and the storm abated.

At another time, with another guide, on the head-waters of the Arkansas, after traveling all day in a terrible storm, they reached a small river for camp, but without a stick of wood anywhere to be had except on the other side of the stream, which was covered with ice, but too thin to support a man erect. The storm cleared away, and the night bid fair to be intensely cold; besides, they must have fire to prepare bread and food. The doctor took his ax in one hand and a willow stick in the other, laid himself upon the thin ice, and spreading his arms and legs, he worked himself over on his breast, cut his wood and slid it over, and returned in the same way.

That was the last time the doctor enjoyed the luxury of his ax—so indispensable at that season of the year, in such a country. That night a wolf poked his nose under the foot of the bed where the ax had been placed for safe-keeping, and took it off for a leather string that had been wrapped around the split helve.

DR. WHITMAN'S SUCCESSFUL MISSION AT WASHINGTON.

On reaching the settlements, Dr. Whitman found that many of the now old Oregonians—Waldo, Applegate, Hamtree, Keyser and others—who had once made calculations to come to Oregon, had abandoned the idea because of the representations from Washington that every attempt to take wagons and ox teams through the Rocky and Blue Mountains to the Columbia had failed. Dr. Whitman saw at once what the stopping of wagons at Fort Hall every year meant. The representations purported to come from Secretary Webster, but really from Governor Simpson, who, magnifying the statements of his chief trader, Grant, at Fort Hall, declared the Americans must be going mad, from their repeated fruitless attempts to take wagons and teams through the impassable regions of the Columbia, and that the women and children of those wild fanatics had been saved from a terrible death only by the repeated and philanthropic labors of Mr. Grant, at Fort Hall, in furnishing them with horses. The doctor told these men as he met them that his only object in crossing the mountains in the dead of winter, at the risk of his life, and through untold sufferings, was to take back an American emigration that summer through the mountains to the Columbia with their wagons and their teams. The route was practicable. We had taken our cattle and our families through seven years before. They had nothing to fear; but to be ready on his return. The stopping of wagons at Fort Hall was a Hudson Bay Company scheme to prevent the settling of the country by Americans, till they could settle it with their own subjects from the Selkirk settlement. This news spread like fire through Missouri, as will be seen from Zacrey's statement. The doctor pushed on to Washington and immediately sought an interview with Secretary Webster—both being from the same State—and stated to him the object of his crossing the mountains, and laid before him the great importance of Oregon to the United States. But Mr. Webster lay too near Cape Cod to see things in the same light with his fellow-statesman who had transferred his worldly interests to the Pacific coast. He awarded sincerity to the missionary, but could not admit for a moment that the short residence of six years could give the doctor the knowledge of the country possessed by Governor Simpson, who had almost grown up in the country, and had traveled every part of it, and represents it as one unbroken waste of sand deserts and impassable mountains, fit only for the beaver, the gray bear, and the savage. Besides, he had about traded it off with Governor Simpson, to go into the Ashburton treaty, for a cod-fishery on Newfoundland.

The doctor next sought, through Senator Linn, an interview with President Tyler, who at once appreciated his solicitude and his timely representations of Oregon, and especially his disinterested though hazardous undertaking to cross the Rocky Mountains in the winter to take back a caravan of wagons. He said that, although the doctor's representations of the character of the country, and the possibility of reaching it by wagon route, were in direct contradiction to those of Governor Simpson, his frozen limbs were sufficient proof of his sincerity, and his missionary character was sufficient guarantee for his honesty, and he would, therefore, as President, rest upon these and act accordingly; would detail Frémont with a military force to escort the doctor's caravan through the mountains; and no more action should be had toward trading off Oregon till he could hear the result of the expedition. If the doctor could establish a wagon route through the mountains to the Columbia River, pronounced impossible by Governor Simpson and Ashburton, he would use his influence to hold on to Oregon. The great desire of the doctor's American soul, Christian withal, that is, the pledge of the President that the swapping of Oregon with England for a cod-fishery should stop for the present, was attained, although at the risk of life, and through great sufferings, and unsolicited, and without the promise or expectation of a dollar's reward from any source. And now, God giving him life and strength, he would do the rest, that is, connect the Missouri and Columbia rivers with a wagon track so deep and plain that neither national envy nor sectional fanaticism would ever blot it out. And when the 4th of September, 1843, saw the rear of the doctor's caravan of nearly two hundred wagons with which he started from Missouri last of April, emerge from the western shades of the Blue Mountains upon the plains of the Columbia, the greatest work was finished ever accomplished by one man for Oregon on this coast. And through that great emigration, during that whole summer, the doctor was their everywhere-present angel of mercy, ministering to the sick, helping the weary, encouraging the wavering, cheering the mothers, mending wagons, setting broken bones, hunting stray oxen; climbing precipices, now in the rear, now in the center, now at the front; in the rivers looking out fords through the quicksands, in the deserts looking out water; in the dark mountains looking out passes; at noontide or midnight, as though those thousands were his own children, and those wagons and those flocks were his own property. Although he asked not and expected not a dollar as a reward from any source, he felt himself abundantly rewarded when he saw the desire of his heart accomplished, the great wagon route over the mountains established, and Oregon in a fair way to be occupied with American settlements and American commerce. And especially he felt himself doubly paid, when, at the end of his successful expedition, and standing alive at his home again on the banks of the Walla-Walla, these thousands of his fellow summer pilgrims, wayworn and sunbrowned, took him by the hand and thanked him with tears for what he had done.

During the doctor's absence his flour mill, with a quantity of grain, had been burned, and consequently he found but a small supply at his station on his return raised by Mr. Geiger, a young missionary. But what he had in the way of grain, garden vegetables, and cattle, he gladly furnished the needy emigrants at the very low figure of the Willamette prices, which was six hundred per cent lower than what they had been compelled to pay at Forts Hall and Boise, and one-half lower than they are to-day in the same country. And this was his practice every year till himself and wife and fourteen emigrants were murdered, in the fall of 1847, because, as General Bramlette says, "they were American citizens," and not, as I am bold to say and can prove, because he was a physician. Shame on the American that will intimate such a thing. The general, who is the vicar-general of the papal hosts on this coast, does not thank you for such an excuse. He tells you plainly it was to break up the American settlements on this coast.

Often the good doctor would let every bushel of his grain go to the passing emigrants in the fall, and then would have to depend upon me for breadstuffs for the winter and the whole year till next harvest for his own large family and the scores of emigrants who every year were obliged to stop at his station on account of sickness or given-out teams. Although the doctor had done so much for his country, it seems his blood was necessary to arouse the Government to take formal possession of this coast; as it was his death by savages that sent the devoted J. L. Meek over the mountains to Washington in the spring of 1848, to beg the Government, in behalf of the citizens of this coast, to send us help and to extend its jurisdiction over us. That prayer was answered by act of Congress, approved August 14, 1848.—*Lecture by Rev.H.H.Spalding.*

GENERAL LOVEJOY'S TESTIMONY — WHITMAN SWIMMING—ICE FLOATING—GRAND RIVER—MERCURY 30 DEGREES BELOW ZERO.

I was the traveling companion of Doctor Whitman in that arduous and trying journey, but at this late hour it will be almost impossible to give many of the thrilling scenes and hair-breadth escapes we went through, traveling, as we did, almost the entire route, through a hostile Indian country, and suffering from the snows and the intense cold. We started, October 3, 1842, and reached Fort Hall in 11 days. Took a southern route via Taos and Santa Fé. From Fort Hall to Fort Winter we met with terribly severe weather. The deep snows caused us to lose much time. Here we took a new guide for Fort Macumpagna, on Grand River, in Spanish country. Passing over high mountains, we encountered a terrible snow storm, that compelled us to seek shelter in a dark defile, and although we made several attempts we were detained some ten days, when we got upon the mountains and wandered for days, when the guide declared he was lost, and would take us no further. This was a terrible blow to the doctor. But he determined not to give it up, and returned to the fort for another guide, I remaining with the horses, feeding them on cotton-wood bark. The seventh day he returned. We reached, as our guide informed us, Grand River, 600 yards wide, which was frozen on either side about one-third. The guide regarded it too dangerous; but the doctor, nothing daunted, was the first to take the water. He mounted his horse, and the guide and myself pushed them off the ice into the boiling, foaming stream. Away they went, completely under water, horse and all, but directly came up, and after buffeting the waves and foaming current, he made for the ice on the opposite side, a long way down the stream—leaped upon the ice, and soon had his noble animal by his side. The guide and I forced in the pack animals, and followed the doctor's example, and were soon drying our frozen clothes by a comfortable fire. We reached Taos in about 30 days. We suffered from intense cold, and from want of food, compelled to use the flesh of dogs, mules, or such other animals as came in our reach. We remained about 15 days, and left for Bent's Fort, which we reached 3d January. The doctor left here on the 7th, at which time we parted, and I did not meet him again till above Laramie, in July. on his way to Oregon with a train of emigrants.

I have no doubt the doctor's interviews with the President and others resulted greatly to the benefit of Oregon and the entire coast.

A. L. LOVEJOY.

Wm. H. Cray, Esq.

DISINTERESTED PATRIOTISM OF THE MARTYR WHITMAN.

Let it not be forgotten that our republic is indebted to the enlightened patriotism of Marcus Whitman, who heroically defied the dangers of a winter's journey across the continent, and by the communication of important facts to our Government prevented the cession of a large portion of our Pacific domain to Great Britain.

A. L. LINDSLEY, D. D., Moderator.
E. R. GEARY, Clerk.

Oregon Presbytery, *Pacific Coast.*

WHITMAN NOT AN HOUR TOO SOON—HON. ELWOOD EVANS'S TESTIMONY.

There is no doubt that the arrival of Dr. Whitman was opportune. The President was satisfied that the Territory was worth the effort to save it. The delay incident to a transfer of negotiations to London was fortunate, for there is reason to believe that if formal negotiations had been renewed in Washington, and that for the sake of settlement of the protracted controversy, and the only remaining unadjudicated cause of difference between the two governments, had the offer been renewed of the 49th parallel to the Columbia, and thence down that river to the Pacific Ocean, it would have been accepted. The visit of Whitman committed the President against any such settlement at that time.—*Hon. Elwood Evans.*

DANIEL WEBSTER ALLEGES THAT WHITMAN SAVED THE PACIFIC WEST.

A martyr of civilization.—We are beginning somewhat to appreciate our Great West, and to hold in deserved regard those pioneers of civilization who opened to us its wonderful possibilities. One of those pioneers, however, whose life was sacrificed to his patriotic zeal, has not, it seems to us, received the honor which his services and sufferings merit. It is not as widely known as it should be, that an important part of our territory beyond the Rocky Mountains was finally secured to the United States by the efforts of Dr. Marcus Whitman.   *   *   *   *   *

A personal friend of Mr. Webster, a legal gentleman, and with whom he conversed on the subject several times, remarked to the writer of this article: "It is safe to assert that our country owes it to Dr. Whitman and his associate missionaries that all the territory west of the Rocky Mountains, and south as far as the Columbia River, is not now owned by England, and held by the Hudson's Bay Company.—*New York Independent, January*, 1870.

WHITMAN AND THIS HEROIC WOMAN LOST THEIR LIVES FOR THEIR COUNTRY WEST
OF THE ROCKY MOUNTAINS.

In confirmation of this opinion (that the Protestant missionary Whitman saved the country) we find a writer in the Colonial Magazine using this language: " By a strange and unpardonable oversight of the local officers, missionaries from the United States were allowed to take religious charge of the population, (Indians,) and these artful men lost no time in introducing such a number of their countrymen as to reduce the influence of the British settlers to complete iusignificance." Whitman had disappointed their gigantic schemes and the disappointment was severe. It is not too much, then, to say that Doctor Whitman and Mrs. Whitman and Mrs. Spalding lost their lives in consequence of the endeavors above described.—*Missionary Herald, December*, 1866.

An unyielding purpose was formed by Doctor Whitman to go East. Mr. Walker and myself were decidedly opposed; Mr. Spalding was in favor and we yielded only when it became evident that he would go even if he had to become disconnected from the mission to do so. Extravagant language has been used expressive of the confidence of the emigrants of 1843 in his ability to conduct them through difficulties which, in the estimation of many, were regarded as utter impossibilities.—*Rev. Dr. Ellis, Associate Missionary of Dr. Whitman.*

Senator Benton said on the Senate floor in 1825: "The child is born who will see the commerce of the Indies concentrating in American cities on the Pacific shores, climbing the Rocky Mountains, rolling down their eastern slopes to enrich and enlarge our Atlantic cities."

And Isaiah hath said: "Until the spirit be found upon us from on high and the waste region be a fruitful field."

Crossing the continent in 1836, when not a single wheel had crushed the wild sage of the desert, and that, too, as an exile—voluntary, to be sure, but none the less an exile--from the land of schools, churches, and home, to the depths of an unknown wilderness, was a very different thing from what, twenty years later, it was found to be by the hundreds and thousands who traveled the same path without even thinking it was missionary zeal that opened the easy way they were then treading. The writer has followed nearly every step of the way thus promised for him, and with wonder and amazement at the courage, the faith, and the hope of the evangel band, who long before were the *avant couriers* of religion and happiness to the land where now he dwells. Mrs. Whitman and Mrs. Spalding, fresh from the homes of refinement, with the dew of their love still sparkling on their eyelids, yet with the courage of martyrs and the faith of saints traveled that long wearisome way, the first commissioned angels of mercy to the land beyond the mountains slumbering in the night of heathen ages.—*Rev. H. K. Hines, in Ladies' Repository.*

The 4th day of July, 1836, our missionary party found themselves in South Pass, the line that divides the waters of the Atlantic from those of the Pacific. And when we remember that these noble missionaries passed these gates of the Rocky Mountains six years before J. C. Frémont discovered this South Pass, we have another illustrious proof of the fact that grace is mightier than cupidity to lead men and women forth from the limits of the seen to the mysterious and adventurous unknown. The day before reaching rendezvous, the missionaries were overjoyed to meet a company of Indians from the far-off Nes Perces country. They had come to meet the missionaries, in fulfillment of a promise made to Dr. Whitman the year before, and here, near a thousand miles from the end of their journey, to welcome and aid them forward. The chiefs were invited to the missionary board that night, and here commenced the friendship of that nation that bound them to the American people and Government through all the conflicts of subsequent years. There, about thirty miles southwest of what is known as Frémont's Peak, and forty west of the summit of the Rocky Mountains, were forged by Christian love those chains that bind the heart of that nation, the noblest, truest, bravest, and most devoted of all the tribes of the interior of our continent to the Americans to this day. Three or four hundred mountain men and perhaps two thousand Indians had gathered at the rendezvous, and for several days this valley of the Colorado was the scene of the wildest excitement. The appearance of two cultivated and talented white women in this fierce throng was like the rising of a new day to the wild adventurers of the chase and the scout. They were the living images of distant mothers and sisters, and as these bronzed men looked upon them tears suffused their eyes. The piety, intelligence, and kindness of those missionary ladies gave lavish contribution of happiness to these dreary hearts. Seventeen years later one of these men related to me, "from that day I was a better man." On the 31st day of August, 1836, the mission band emerged from the timbered depths of the Blue Mountains, and stood on an elevated prairie summit overlooking the great valley of the Middle Columbia. The deserts and the wilderness were passed. Unknown to statesmen and really intent only in filling the measure of high religious consecration, these wives had solved the problem of the future of the land which God now showed them. The prayers, the songs, of that evening were like those of Moses, on Nebo, or Miriam, at the Red Sea crossing.

These prayers jarred principalities and powers. These songs were a prophesy fulfilled, fulfilling, and to be fulfilled over a land then greeting unconsciously the dawning of the day of American civilization.

In the fall of 1842 it became apparent to Dr. Whitman, from oft conversations with gentlemen of the Hudson's Bay Company, and from the sudden arrival of a colony of one hundred and forty souls from the Hudson's Bay settlement on the Red River of the North, to settle permanently on these Pacific shores, that a deep laid plan was about to culminate successfully to secure the title to Oregon to Great Britain. He astonished his family, the mission, and all the whites in the country, by the announcement of his determination to proceed at once to Washington and thwart, if possible, that design. To cross the Rocky Mountains in the deep winter, to brave the cold, to meet the storms of the mountain deserts, to dare almost unattended the dangers of savage ambush were to them fearful facts; to him, only the necessary incidents in the consummation of his grand and patriotic conception. His wife alone, of all around with whom he could advise, seemed capable of rising to the lofty idea. These two great minds comprehended the issues of the hour. They saw the deprivations, and toils, and trials of the present, bringing forth fruit of wealth, and rest, and safety to a nation of freemen soon to swarm through the valleys of the Pacific. Which exhibited the greater heroism, he in encountering the fearful perils of that journey through the mountains of Utah and New Mexico, or she in remaining almost alone among the savages of the northwest coast for the year of his absence, it is difficult to tell. Both acts rise into the morally sublime. On the arrival of Dr. Whitman in Washington, 2d March, 1843, he found he had not started one day too soon to save the northwest coast of the United States. The Webster-Ashburton treaty, by which the United States were to relinquish to England the title to that part of Oregon north of the Columbia, was about to be executed. On his representations of the value of the country, and of the practicability of a wagon road across the continent to the Columbia, the President hesitated, but when these representations were enforced by the fact that the doctor's own wife, accompanied by only one white lady companion, had already crossed the continent and were now in the valley of the Walla-Walla, lone representatives of Christianity and American civilization, he hesitated no longer, but adopted that course of action which resulted in securing to the United States the title to Oregon up to 49°, and will eventually give us the whole of the northwest coast.

Once more crossing the continent at the head of the first emigration to the shores of the Pacific, baffling the armed hostility of savages, and the wily stratagems of the officers of the Hudson's Bay Company, that great British monopoly which had so long ruled over the plains of the Columbia, and which dreaded the presence and rivalry of simple American citizens. Dr. Whitman again reached his beloved Waiilatpu, his mission home upon the banks of the Walla-Walla, in the autumn of 1843. By those whom he had led to the country he was regarded now, not as a missionary merely, but as well a statesman and a hero; by those whose plans and machinations he had defeated, he was regarded with coldness and distrust.

Without reciting the mournful details of that tragic day which made Waiilatpu forever famous in the annals of missionary martyrdom, we close our record. But history will write on. After ages will pay their due tribute of honor to the brave and Christian men and women who were alike the founders of empire and the servants of Christ. Missionary zeal will relume its ardor at the mention of Waiilatpu, and with a mightier consecration to the faith, go forth conquering and to conquer.

On the banks of the Walla-Walla, in a lowly grave, unmarked by an inscription, the mortal remains of Dr. and Mrs. Whitman are slumbering away the years. They sleep not far from the spot where the consecrated years of their mature life were so lavishly given to that noblest of all work, raising the fallen and saving the lost. Living, they were the peers of such heroes and heroines as Dr. and Ann Hasseletine Judson; and dying, their memory is entitled to the same enshrinement in the grateful regards of a Church and State, indebted to them for one of the finest illustrations of unselfish patriotism and of the purity and power of ancient faith. And when He whom they served with such special devotion shall assemble His best beloved, they of the eastern shall greet those of the western shore of the Pacific, and hail them fellow heirs to martyr's robe and crown.—*Rev. H. K. Hines, of Fort Vancouver, Washington Territory, in Ladies' Repository for September, 1868.*

WHITMAN'S REPORT IN FEBRUARY, 1843—COLLECTS ONE THOUSAND SOULS FROM
WESTERN STATES.

BROWNSVILLE, *February* 7, 1868,

DEAR SIR: In answer to your inquiries, I would say that my father and his family emigrated to Oregon in 1843, from the State of Texas. I was then 17 years old. The occasion of my father starting that season for this country, as also several of our neighbors, was a publication by Dr. Whitman, or from his representations, concerning Oregon and the route from the States to Oregon. In the pamphlet the doctor described Oregon, the soil, climate, and its desirableness for Americon colonies, and said that he had crossed the Rocky Mountains that winter principally to take back that season a train of wagons to Oregon. We had been told that wagons could not be taken beyond Fort Hall. But in this pamphlet the doctor assured his countrymen that wagons could be taken through from Fort Hall to the Columbia River, and to the Dalles, and from thence by boats to the Willamette; that himself and mission party had taken their families, cattle, and wagons through to the Columbia, six years before. It was this assurance of the missionary that induced my father and several of his neighbors to sell out and start at once for this country.

The doctor was of great service to the emigrants as physician, and in looking out fords in the Platte and passes in the mountains. At Fort Hall the officers of the Hudson's Bay Company told us we could never get our wagons and families through to Oregon, we must go to California. The Hudson's Bay Company would not allow Americans to settle in Oregon. Dr. Whitman told us if we would trust him, he would see that we reached the Dalles by 20th September. We did trust him, and most faithfully did he make his word good, and in many ways did he render most invaluable service to the emigration. Agreeably to instructions which the doctor had left with his Indians the year before, Stickus, a Cayuse chief, and his young men, met the doctor between Bear River and Fort Hall, and staid with us, and were of great service in looking out the route through the Blue Mountains, every foot of which ground these Indians were acquainted with. Stickus would ride down two or three horses in a day, looking out the best passes. These were the first wagons and teams to pass through these mountains. Dr. Whitman furnished us with an Indian guide from his mission station to the Dalles without charge. He advised us all to go on to the Willamette. He furnished us with beef and flour at Willamette prices.

JOHN ZACHREY.

Rev. H. H. SPALDING.

V.—THE WHITMAN MASSACRE AND THE ATTEMPT TO BREAK UP THE AMERICAN SETTLEMENTS.

After visiting the sick in the Indian camp on the Umatilla, Dr. Whitman took tea with Bishop Blanchette and General Brouilette, who had arrived at the Umatilla on Saturday. The general assured him that he would be over to Waiilatpu on Tuesday. The doctor returned to our camp about sundown; was much encouraged, and thought that we had everything to hope from the Brouilette visit on Tuesday. The severe sickness at home made it necessary for the doctor to return that night, and although more fit for a bed of rest, from his increasing labors and cares, he took me by the hand and bade me farewell, more hopeful than I had seen him, (and Brouilette refers to this; O, the wretch that could create a false hope to make human anguish the deeper,) mounted his borrowed mule, gave whip, and was out of sight. Eighteen years have passed away and I have seen him no more, and shall not till I meet him, by the grace of our Lord, in the streets of the New Jerusalem, where are no more deaths and all tears are wiped away. He had about twenty-eight miles to ride, and did not reach his home till the dawn of the 29th—the bloody 29th of November, 1847. And now I come to the details of that and the eight following bloody days. And my heart sickens and my hand trembles even at this late date, as I attempt to portray that bloody tragedy; not so much on account of the fearful, terrible work of the immediate agents, the naked painted savages; strong men, young men, American citizens, fathers, husbands, allured, hewed down and ripped open; a husband's heart converted into a foot-ball in sight of a helpless wife, the terrified daughter forced into the arms of the naked savage to be his wife who has just shot down her father who lies gasping at her feet; the helpless women, young women, girls so young, that the knife had to be used, writhing in the hands of unrestrained brutality; hogs and dogs running about with parts of human heads and lungs in their mouths; and—O, my God! has hell swallowed up the earth?—with all, and in the midst of all, the priest of God administering the holy ordinance of baptism upon the blood-stained children of these bloody savages. I say I shudder to attempt a recital, not so much on account of the horrible character of the tragedy as from the conviction that the white man was concerned in it from beginning to end, to break up the American settlements and regain this country. The details of that tragedy, which J.

Ross Browne says involved this country in a twelve years' war, and the causes that appear to have led to it, I have received from eye-witnesses who escaped, from emigrants, from reports of the army, and from the trial of the five Indians who were executed at Oregon City. Much of this testimony is given under the oath of the widows and daughters, who were fearful sufferers, and the few who escaped. I would go to an individual and take down in writing what he or she knew, and then go before a magistrate and the individual would make oath to the statement, the officer certifying.

On arriving at home the doctor and his wife were seen in tears, much agitated. The doctor sent for Findley, a Hudson's Bay half-breed with a Cayuse wife, who lived in a lodge about 100 yards distant. "Findley, I understand the Indians are to kill me and Mr. Spalding; do you know anything about it?" "I should know, doctor; you have nothing to fear; there is no danger." O, the wretch that could thus throw them off their guard! The savages were at that moment in council in his lodge. Early in the morning an Indian came in for a coffin and winding-sheet and the doctor to assist in burying a child. (We always furnished these, and assisted in burying the dead, if possible). On returning from the grave the doctor was much excited, and said to his wife, "What does this mean, only one Indian at the grave, while multitudes are collected on foot and on horse?" But a beef had been brought in, shot down, and was being dressed, and was thought to have been the cause.

It is desirable to describe the premises, and the number of families stopping at the station to winter. The doctor's *adobe* dwelling-house stood on the north bank of Walla-Walla River, 25 miles from Fort Walla-Walla, now Walula, and one-half mile above the mouth of Pusha or Mill Creek, facing west, well finished and furnished with a good library and a large cabinet of choice specimens. Connected with the north end was a large Indian room, and an ell extending from the east seventy feet, consisting of kitchen, sleeping-room, school-room and church. One hundred yards east stood a large *adobe* building. At a point forming a triangle with the above line stood the mill, granary, and shops; a saw-mill and dwelling-house 18 miles up Mill Creek; Fort Colville 200 miles north; the mission station of Revs. Eells and Walker among the Spokane and Flathead Indians 140 miles north; our mission at the Dalles, 175 miles west; my own mission among the Nez Perces on Clearwater, at the mouth of Lapwai, 110 miles east. There were connected with or stopping at the Waiilatpu or Whitman station seventy-two souls, mostly American immigrants on their way from the States to the Willamette Valley, stopping to winter, distributed as follows: At the saw-mill, Mr. and Mrs. Young and 3 grown-up sons, from Missouri; Mr. and Mrs. Smith and 5 children—eldest daughter, 16—from Illinois. In the blacksmith shop, Mr. Canfield, wife and 5 children, eldest daughter of 16, from Iowa. In the large building, Mr. Kimball, wife and 5 children, eldest daughter of 16, from Indiana; Mr. Hall, wife and 5 children, eldest a daughter of 10, from Illinois; Mr. Saunders, wife and 5 children, eldest a daughter of 14, from Iowe; Mrs. Hays and child; Mr. Marsh and daughter, and Mr. Gill, tailor. In the Indian room, Mr. Osborne, wife and 3 children, from Oregon, all sick. The Doctor's family consisted of 22 persons, viz, himself and wife, Mr. Rogers, a missionary, seven adopted children of one family by the name of Sager, whose parents had died on the plains in 1844; 3 adopted half-breed children, one a daughter of the mountaineer Bridger, one a daughter of J. L. Meek, and a half breed Spanish boy; Miss Bewley, a pious young lady of 23, sick up stairs, and her brother and Mr. Sails, both sick in the sleeping-room; Mr. Hoffman, of New York; J. Stanfield, a Canadian; Lewis, the Catholic half-breed; two half-breed boys and my own daughter Eliza, 10 years of age, in the school-room. Mr. Marsh was running the mill; Mr. Hall was laying a floor in the cook-room; Mr. Saunders teaching the school, which was just taken up for the afternoon; Messrs. Hoffman, Kimball and Canfield were dressing the beef between the mill and blacksmith shop; Mr. Rogers upon the river bank; John, eldest of the Sager family, and the Bridger girl, lay in the kitchen sick; the doctor, his wife, Catherine Sager, 13 years old, in the sitting-room with three very sick children.

The Indians, with weapons concealed under their blankets, were ready at all these points, waiting a signal from Joe Lewis, who stood at the south door watching both the doctor and those without. Mrs. Osborne, for the first time in six weeks, had stepped upon the floor, and stood talking with Mrs. Whitman near the sick children. An Indian opened the kitchen door and called to the doctor for medicine, who accordingly went in and sat down by the Indian, and administered a potion to him.

While the sick Indian engrossed the doctor's attention, Tamahos stepped behind him, drew a pipe tomahawk from under his blanket, and buried it in the doctor's head. He fell partly forward, and a second blow on the back of the head brought him to the floor. The Indian had to put his foot on the doctor's head to tear the tomahawk out, and said: "I have killed my father." With the first blow upon the doctor's head, the terrible work commenced on all sides at the same time. John Sager, lying sick in the same room, made some defense, but was shot in several places and his throat cut, and the body thrown partly across Dr. Whitman. Mrs. Osborne says, immediately after the doctor went into the kitchen, an Indian opened the door, spoke in native to Mrs. W., who had only time to raise her hands, and exclaim: "Oh, my God!" when the guns fired, and the crash of weapons and the yells commenced.   We can describe the scene at but one point at once.   Four Indians stood around Mr. Gill, the tailor, in the large house, weapons concealed, awaiting the signal.   Three shots were fired at him, but one taking effect, breaking his back.   The sufferer lingered in great agony, begging the women to shoot him in the head, and expired about 12 o'clock.   The women naturally ran to the doctor's house, meeting savages naked, painted, yelling, laughing, frantic, hewling, cutting down their victims everywhere.   As they came into the kitchen, Mrs. W. was attempting to move her husband.   John was gasping.   The Bridger girl was covered with blood and seemed dead, but it was the blood from Dr. W.   Next day she was found alive.   Sails and Bewley, who lay sick in next door, were groaning terribly, but next day were found unwounded.   Mrs. Hall, who stopped to assist Mrs. Whitman, says: "The doctor's ribs were smashed."   They dragged him into the sitting-room, and applied a bag of hot ashes to stop the blood.   Mrs. W., kneeling over her gasping husband, said: "Doctor, do you know me?"   The dying missionary was to speak no more; he only moved his lips.   The dear wife saw her terrible fate.   She raised herself and exclaimed, "Oh, God, thy will be done!   I am left a widow.   Oh, may my parents never know this!"   The Indians seemed to have left the house.   The terrible scene without—the roar of guns, the crash of war clubs and tomahawks, the groans of the dying, the screams of women, the howling of dogs, the yells of the savage demons, naked, painted with black and white—naturally attracted the attention of Mrs. Whitman, and she stepped to a south window, but instantly raised her hands and exclaimed, "Joe, is this you doing all this?" and the glass rattled. She fell, the bullet having passed through her right breast.   She lay some time apparently dead, when she revived so as to speak; and her first words, before she could raise her head, her heart's blood fast running away and mingling with the blood of her gasping husband and two others who had been brought in wounded, were a prayer: "Oh, my Saviour, take care of my children, now to be left a second time orphans and among Indians."   Joe Lewis was undoubtedly the one who shot Mrs. Whitman, and who took the lead in this bloody tragedy; and but for him, his teasing the Indians, and his false representations, the Indians would never have killed their best friends and butchered the Americans.   He told the writer he was born in Canada and educated in Maine.   He was a good scholar and good mechanic, and had the appearance of an eastern half-breed, spoke the English and his native tongue and was a devoted Catholic, wearing his cross and counting his beads often.   The emigrants of that year saw him first at Fort Hall, and Mrs. Lee testifies that he was several times heard to say, "There will be a change in that country (Walla-Walla) when the Fathers get down."   He told the Indians that he was a Chinook; that the Americans had stolen him when a child.   He had grown up in America; knew the Americans, hated the Indians, and intended to exterminate them; would send missionaries first, and then the multitude would come and take the country.   They had better kill Dr. Whitman and the missionaries, and what Americans there were; they could do it, and he would help them.   They would receive plenty of ammunition from below. After the butchery, he was protected as never an American was; went off with most of the money and valuables plundered from the helpless widows and orphans, and has been seen at the northeast stations; was evidently engaged in Canada to do this work, as he came over with the party from Europe.

Mr. Canfield, one of the three dressing the beef, who escaped, and finally reached my station, in the country of the Nez Perce Indians, says: " We saw multitudes of Indians collecting on foot and horse, but thought it was on account of the beef.   The first notice was a shock like terrific peals of thunder, accompanied by an unearthly yell of the savages.   I sprang up, but saw ourselves perfectly enveloped by naked Indians, whose guns seemed blazing in our faces.   I turned twice before I saw an opening; saw Mr. Kimball fall; sprang for the opening, and through the thick smoke, dashing the guns aside with my hands.   At a little distance I looked back and saw an Indian taking aim at me, and afterward found that a ball had entered my back and passed around between the skin and ribs, where it remains.   I passed my family in the shop, and catching up a child, ran into the large building, up stairs, and into the garret, where I looked down from the window upon the whole scene.   Saw the naked savages painted black and white, yelling and leaping like flying demons, caps of eagle feathers streaming, guns roaring, tomahawks, war clubs, and knives, brandishing over the heads of their victims; white women running and screaming, and the Indian women singing and dancing.   Saw Kimball run around the north end of the doctor's house, covered with blood, and one arm swinging, pursued by Indians.   Saw Hoffman fall several times, but would rise amid the flying tomahawks, till he was backed up in the corner of the doctor's house, when two Indians came up on horses with long-handled tomahawks, over-reached, cut him down, and he rose no more.   Saw some Indians apparently trying to protect our women and children.   Saw Mr. Rogers run into the house from the river, with one arm swinging, and pursued by four Indians; also saw Mrs. Saunders, led by two Indians, go into Findley's lodge.   Saw Joe Lewis and a whole crowd of Indians and Indian women driving our school children from the school door into the kitchen, with tomahawks, guns, and knives brandishing over their little heads and in their faces. My heart fainted for them, but I could do nothing. Paid Joe Stanfield a watch to bring me a horse to a given point of brush after dark. Went there and waited all night, but no horse came."

Four Indians attacked Mr. Hall lying on the floor in the cook-room; the first gun missed fire, when Mr. Hall wrenched the gun from the Indian, and they ran, giving him time to reach the brush, where he lay till dark, and that night found his way to Fort Walla-Walla, but was turned out, put over the Columbia River, and has never been heard from since. It is said he was immediately killed by the Indians. There were in the fort, besides the gentlemen in charge, some twenty white men, including some ten Catholic priests, who had arrived in the country about six weeks before, under the immediate superintendency of Bishop Blanchett and Vicar General Brouilette, a part via Cape Horn and part by the overland route. It is reported that the children of Mr. Hall, after their arrival at the fort, saw the pants, cap, and sash of their father. As the roar and yells commenced, Mr. Saunders, the teacher, naturally opened the school-room door, when three Indians came up the steps and seized him. His daughter Helen and my daughter Eliza ran to the window. Helen screamed, "They are killing my father." Eliza gazed a few minutes on the terrible scene. She saw Mr. Saunders fall and rise several times among the tomahawks and knives, trying to reach his house, till two Indians came up on horses, and with long-handled tomahawks hewed him down. Next day in going among the dead she found his head split open, a part lying at a distance; and with her tender hands the dear child put it in its place, and assisted in sewing sheets around his and the other bodies. She found Hoffman split open in the back, and his heart and lungs taken out; she replaced them, and sewed a sheet around him. His afflicted sister, in Elmira, New York, writes me, "I desire above all things to clasp that dear child to my bosom before I die, for her kindness to my fallen brother, whom I am to see no more." Eliza saw multitudes of Indian women and children dancing, and naked men swinging their hatchets dripping with blood.

In the sitting-room there were now four persons bleeding, Dr. and Mrs. Whitman, Kimball, and Rogers; Sager was in the kitchen. After the women came in, they fastened the doors and took the sick children and Mrs. W. up stairs. At the commencement the children of the school hid themselves in the loft over the school-room. Toward night Findley, Joe Lewis, and several Indians came in, and called to the children to come down. Findley selected the two Manson (Hudson Bay) boys and the doctor's Spanish boy, to take to Walla-Walla, to save their lives, and said the others were to be killed by the Indian women. My Eliza caught Findley by the clothes: "Oh, Nicholas, save me, do!" He pushed her away, and Lewis and the Indians huddled them down into the kitchen. As they were driven into the kitchen to be shot, they passed over the body of John. His brother Francis, fifteen years old, stooped down, took the woolen scarf from the gory thoat of his dying brother, and spoke to him. John gasped, and immediately expired. Francis said to his sister Matilda, "I shall go next," and was never heard to speak again. The children were huddled in a corner, where a scene that beggars description commenced. The large room filled up with Indian women and naked, painted men, yelling, dancing, scraping up the blood that was deep upon the floor, and flirting it, painting their guns, and brandishing their bloody tomahawks over the heads of these helpless little lambs, screaming, "Shall we shoot? Shall we shoot?" Eliza, who could understand the language, says, "I covered my eyes with my apron, that I might not see the bloody tomahawk strike that was just over my head." Telankaikt, the head chief, (who was hung at Oregon City,) stood in the door to give the order. In this fearful situation these dear children were held for an hour. Those spared are now grown-up women and men, and scattered over this coast, and must ever look back upon that hour with the deepest emotions, as affording a striking proof on the one hand of the malignant, unfit state of the human, unrenewed heart for the purity of heaven, and, on the other, of the interposing hand of Heaven. Ups and Moolpod, the doctor's Indian herdsmen, crawled in, threw their robes around the children, and huddled them out of the north door into the corner. But here the Indians, who seemed to have finished up the bloody work elsewhere, soon collected in great numbers, arranging themselves three or four deep the whole length of the seventy-foot ell, with their guns drawn and pointing to the same door. This would bring the children, now huddled in the corner, in range.

About this time Canfield saw Joe Lewis at the head of a band of Indians break in the south door of the doctor's house with his gun. They came into the sitting-room, broke down the stair door, and were coming up stairs. The women collected around Mrs. Whitman, who lay bleeding. "The Indians are coming; we are to die; but are not prepared. What shall we do?" The gasping saint with her dying breath replied earnestly and calmly, "Go to Jesus and ask him, and He will save you." Thus the faithful missionary spent her last breath, who entered the church at the early age of thirteen. Some one said, "Put that old gun-barrel over the stairway to frighten them." Mrs. W. replied, "Let all prepare to die." Mr. Rogers went to the head of the stairs, spoke to Tomsuekey, who said: "The young men have done this; they will burn the house to-night; you had better all come down and go over to the big house, where we will take care of you." Oh, the demon, that could thus throw them off their guard at the last moment! Eliza, just out among the children, could hear all this, and knew now what the Indians, arranged along the house with their guns drawn, were waiting for. Fearful moments for the dear child, as she heard the steps down stairs and approaching the fatal door, but of course could give no warning. Mr. Kimball, Catherine, Elizabeth, and the sick children remained in the chamber. Mr. Rogers, Mrs. Whitman, and Miss Bewley came down. The doctor's face had been terribly cut, after Joe came in, but he was yet breathing slowly. Mrs. W. fainted. Supposing she was to be saved, she had told them to get some clothing from the bed-room. They laid her upon a settee, and Joe and Mr. Rogers took the settee, passed into the kitchen, Miss Bewley ahead, over the body of John, out of the kitchen door, and about the length of the settee, when Mr. Rogers saw his doom, and both dropped the settee. Mr. R. had only time to raise his hands and exclaim, "My God, have mercy!" when the guns fired. An Indian seized Francis by the hair of the head, while Lewis jerked one of his pistols from his belt, put the muzzle to Francis' neck and fired, blowing the whole charge into the boy's throat. Mr. Rogers fell upon his face; Mrs. Whitman, Mr. Rogers, and Francis were all three shot in several places, but not killed. The balls flew all about the children, riddling their clothes. One passed through Miss Bewley's clothes and burned her fingers, but none of them were hit. The smoke, blood and brains flew over them, as they stood trembling and silent with terror. Several naked savages gathered around Miss Bewley with tomahawks drawn over head, but when she stopped screaming they led her away to the large house.

And now commenced a scene beyond the reach of the pen, and which must convince any unprejudiced mind that there is a hell in the human heart, if nowhere else. The poor helpless children were compelled to witness it. The Indian women and children were particularly active—yelling, dancing, and singing the scalp-dance. Mrs. Whitman was thrown violently from the settee into the mud. They tried to ride their horses over the bodies, but the horses refused. They slashed the faces of their dying victims with their whips, and as they would writhe and groan, it only increased the glee of the Indian women and children. They leaped and screamed for joy, throwing handsful of blood around, and drinking down the dying agonies of their victims as a precious draft. These blood-stained little savages were to receive the sacred ordinance of baptism a few hours after at the hands of the priest of God—the mangled bodies yet lying unburied around him, the food of dogs and wolves by night and of hogs and vultures by day, seemingly as pay down to the Indians for what they had done. The face of the sun had withdrawn from the sight, and the shades of night were settling upon the once beautiful valley of the Walla-Walla, for ages unknown the home and burying-place of the red man, but now to pass into the hands of another race by this covenant of the missionaries' blood. The children were led over to the large house. The yells of the savages died away. The horrible scene was changed from the dead and dying to the living and helpless, and became more terrific because death could not come to the relief of the sufferers. Helpless women and daughters, with their husbands and fathers dead or dying in sight, young girls so young the knife had to be used, subjected to the brutalities of the naked, painted demons, four or five at a time glutting their hell-born passions upon one of these most to be pitied of our fellow mortals.

And all this, which ought to call forth the undying sympathies of every true American, is made more intolerable to the surviving sufferers by being made, the last few years, the subject of scoffs and jeers, or cold rebuffs, by those receiving extensive patronage from Government and the public.

The three sufferers yet breathing continued to groan on till in the night, as heard by Mr. Osborne and family, who lay concealed under the floor near by. The voice of Francis ceased first, then Mrs. Whitman, and last Mr. Rogers was heard to say, "Come, Lord Jesus, come quickly," and was heard no more. Thus fell at her post the devoted Mrs. Whitman, daughter of Judge Prentiss, of Prattsburg, New York, alone, under the open heavens, no mother's hand or husband's voice to soothe her last moments—the cold earth her dying pillow, her own blood her winding sheet. The companion of my youth, we were members of the same school, of the same church, of the same hazardous journey, of the same mission. Rest, sweet dust, till Jesus shall gather up the scattered members.

> Away from her home and the friends of her youth,
> She hasted, the herald of mercy and truth;
> For the love of the Lord, and to seek for the lost,
> Soon, alas! was her fall, but she died at her post.
>
> She wept not herself that her warfare was done;
> The battle was fought and the victory won;
> But she whispered of those whom her heart clung to most—
> "Tell my sisters for me that I died at my post."

And thus fell, not a "St. Bernard," nor yet an Oberlin, but Whitman, Oregon's Whitman, the yearly emigrant's own Whitman; emphatically a patriot without guile, a

Christian whose faith was measured by his works; who counted not his life dear unto him if he might but do good to his fellow-beings, white or red, whose forethought, whose hazards, labors, and sufferings, self-devised, unsolicited, unrewarded, to reach Washington through the snows of New Mexico, did more for Oregon and this coast than the labor of any other man. Go, dear brother; your great work is done and well done. Already are fulfilled your remarkable words on the banks of the Umatilla, on that our last night: "My death may do as much good to Oregon as my life can." Only eighteen years have passed away this last November, 1865, and the red man is gone.

> The stranger's eye wept that in life's brightest bloom,
> One gifted so highly should sink to the tomb.
> For ardor he led in the van of the host;
> He fell like a hero, he died at his post.
>
> He asked not a stone to be scuptured with verse,
> He asked not that Fame should his merit rehearse,
> But he asked, as a boon, when he gave up the ghost,
> That his brethren might know he died at his post.

Extensive settlements and a considerable town, schools and Christian churches, daily stages, and the hum of business occupy the valley of the Walla-Walla, which, but for the blood of Whitman, would to-day have been occupied by Indian farms and Cayuse horses. Moreover, it was the death of Whitman that sent J. L. Meek to Washington, in the winter of 1848, as a delegate, to beg Congress to extend its jurisdiction and send us help, which prayer was answered by act of Congress, approved August 14, 1848.

Under the judicious and energetic policy of Doctor Whitman, a double and noble object was accomplished. The way-worn, destitute emigrant, compelled to winter with the doctor, needed employment to procure subsistence and horses to go on the next spring. The Indians needed their lands broken and rails made and had an over-abundance of horses (several chiefs had 1,000 head each) to pay. The doctor set the white man to work for the Indians, received pay from the Indians and paid the whites. In this way the Cayuse were enlarging their improvements every year, and were raising over ten thousand bushels of grain (including peas) yearly, and would soon have been so firmly fixed upon their lands; and promising so well, the Government would never have attempted to move them; and but for the blood of Whitman, the Indians would not have consented. They feel his blood has purchased the country which they have forfeited by his death.

The next day, Edward, son of the chief, and the one who met me to kill me, returned from the Umatilla, as stated by D. Young, and said the white chief advised him to kill all the Americans, and he went up to the saw-mill and was bringing down Mr. and Mrs. Young, Mr. and Mrs. Smith, and their families, to kill them, when Timothy, a Nez Perces chief, and "Eagle," native Christians, arrived from Lapwai, and prevented it by saying no more Americans should be killed while they were alive. No more were killed. There were now fifty women and children writhing in the hands of the bloody savages, and four Americans—Young, and his two remaining sons, and Smith, from the saw-mill. Three sick children died in the hands of the Indians. A child of Mrs Hays and two of the doctor's children, and Mr. Osborne and family, had reached Walla-Walla.

ESCAPE OF MR. OSBORNE AND FAMILY.

The almost miraculous escape of Mr. Osborne, wife and family, their cruel reception at Fort Walla, as given by himself. Mr. Osborne is a worthy citizen of Linn County, Oregon, and a devoted member of the Church of Christ. Mrs. Osborne, after enduring unceasing sufferings for fifteen years from successive ulcer sores around the shoulder, occasioned by her chills and terrific sufferings, has regained her health through a kind Providence.

Mr. Osborne says: "As the guns fired and the yells commenced, I leaned my head upon the bed and committed myself and family to my Maker. My wife removed the loose floor. I dropped under the floor with my sick family in their night-clothes, taking only two woolen sheets, a piece of bread and some cold mush, and pulled the floor over us. In five minutes the room was full of Indians, but they did not discover us. The roar of guns, the yells of the savages, and the crash of the clubs, and the knives, and the groans of the dying, continued till dark. We distinctly heard the dying groans of Mrs. Whitman, Mr. Rogers, and Francis, till they died away, one after the other. We heard Mr. Rogers's last, in a slow voice, 'Come, Lord Jesus, come quickly,' and heard no more. Soon after this I removed the floor, and we went out. We saw the white face of Francis by the door. It was warm, as we laid our hand upon it, but he was dead. I carried my two youngest children, who were sick, and my wife held on to my clothes in her great weakness. We had all been sick with measles. Two infants had died. She had not left her bed for six weeks till that day, when she stood up a few minutes. The naked, painted Indians were dancing the scalp-dance around a large fire at a little distance. There seemed no hope for us, and we knew not which way to go, but we bent our steps toward Fort Walla-Walla. A dense, cold fog shut out every

S. Ex. Doc. 37——3

star, and the darkness was complete. We could see no trail, and not even the hand before the face. We had to feel out the trail with our feet. My wife almost fainted, but staggered along. Mill Creek, which we had to wade, was high from late rains, and came up to the waist. My wife, in her great weakness, came near washing down, but held to my clothes, I bracing myself with a stick, holding a child in one arm. I had to cross five times for the children. The water was icy cold and the air freezing some. Staggering along about two miles, Mrs. Osborne fainted and could go no farther, and we hid ourselves in the brush of the Walla-Walla River, not far below Tom Suckey's (a chief) lodges, who was very active at the commencement of the butchery. We were thoroughly wet, and the cold fog, like snow, was about us.

"The cold mud was partially frozen as we crawled, feeling our way, into the dark brush. We could see nothing, the darkness was so extreme   I spread one wet sheet down on the frozen ground; wife and children crouched upon it. I covered the other over them. I thought they must soon perish, as they were shaking, and their teeth rattling terribly with cold. I kneeled down and commended us to my Maker. The day finally dawned, and we could see Indians riding furiously up and down the trail. Sometimes they would come close to the brush, and our blood would warm and the shaking would stop, from fear, for a moment. The day seemed a week. Expected every moment my wife would breath her last. Tuesday night felt our way to the trail, and staggered along to Sutucks Nima, (Dry Creek,) which we waded as we did the other creek; and kept on about two miles, when my wife fainted, and could go no farther. Crawled into the brush and frozen mud, to shake and suffer on from hunger and cold, without sleep. The children, too, wet and cold, called incessantly for food, but the shock of groans and yells at first so frightened them that they did not speak loud. Wednesday night wife was too weak to stand. I took our second child and started for Walla-Walla; had to wade the Touchet; stopped frequently in the brush from weakness; had not recovered from measles. Heard a horseman pass and repass, as I lay concealed in the willows. Have since learned it was Mr. Spalding. Reached Fort Walla-Walla after daylight; begged Mr. McBean for horses to get my family, for food, blankets and clothing, to take to them, and to take care of my child till I could bring my family in, should I live to find them alive. Mr. McBean told me I could not bring my family to his fort. Mr. Hall had come in on Monday night, but he could not have an American in his fort, and he had put him over the Columbia River; that he could not let me have horses, or anything for my wife and children, and I must go to Umatilla. Insisted on bringing my family to the fort, but he refused; said he would not let us in. I next begged the priests to show pity, as my wife and children must perish, and the Indians would undoubtedly kill me, but with no better success. I then begged to leave my child, who was now safe in the fort, but they refused.

"There were many priests in the fort. Mr. McBean gave me breakfast, but I saved most of it for my family. Providentially, Mr. Stanley, an artist, came in from Colville, narrowly escaped the Cayuse Indians by telling them he was "Alain," H. B. He let me have his two horses, some food he had left from Rev. Eells's and Walker's Mission; also a cap, a pair of socks, a shirt and handkerchief, and Mr. McBean furnished an Indian, who proved most faithful; and Thursday night we started back, taking my child, but with a sad heart, that I could not find mercy at the hands of the priests of God. The Indian guided me in the thick darkness to where I supposed I had left my dear wife and children. We could see nothing, and dare not call aloud. Daylight came and I was exposed to Indians, but we continued to search till I was about to give it up in despair, when the Indian discovered one of the twigs I had broken as a guide in coming out to the trail. Following these he soon found my wife and children, yet alive. I distributed what little food and clothing I had, and we started for the Umatilla, the guide leading the way to a ford. But just as were about to cross, a Cayuse came upon us. I gave him a piece of tobacco. He told my Indian he had come to kill us all. My Indian replied, ' Yes, you had better kill them, you have no scalps now, but then you will have five. The sick man's, this woman's, and the three children's. You will then be big brave.' By this he shamed the Cayuse, who said 'I will not kill them, but they will be killed at Umatilla, and that will do.' He left, and we crossed the Walla-Walla River, and the guide said, ' Go to the fort.' My wife said 'If I am to die, I will die at the door of the white man. We will go to the fort, if God will save us to reach that place.' The Indian had to hold my wife before him on the horse. To escape the Indians, we had to hide in the brush till dark. We reached the fort late Sunday night. I laid my wife down and knocked at the gate. Mr. McBean came, and asked who is there. I replied. He said he could not let us in; we must go to Umatilla, or he would put us over the river, as he had Mr. Hall. My wife replied, 'she would die at the gate, but she would not leave.' He finally opened and took us into a secret room, and sent an allowance of food for us every day. Next day I asked him for blankets for my sick wife to lie on. He had nothing. Next day I urged again. He had nothing to give, but would sell a blanket out of the store. I told him I had lost everything, and had nothing to pay, but if I should live to get to the Willamette, I would pay. He consented. But the hip-bones of my dear wife wore through the skin on the hard floor. Stickus, the chief, came in one day and took the cap from his head and gave it to me, and a handkerchief to my child."

This fort Walla-Walla is one of the "St. Bernards" spoken of so highly by Captain Mullan in his valuable report on his military road, where the destitute and weary are ever treated kindly! Strange kindness. The same Captain Mullen, and some others I shall have occasion to notice, by silence virtually condemned the whole policy of Doctor Whitman, his invaluable labors in first opening the great emigrant route, and again his hazards and sufferings in saving it and this great West to his country, and his unceasing kindness in giving supplies to the passing emigrants, and his great work among the Indians. Not a word in his book about the good man or his many good and great works. A few more such religious fanatics in our Army and Navy and Indian Department, and it would not be difficult to get up another St. Bartholomew in our country.

The sun of the 30th of November refused to shine on the once beautiful and happy valley of the Walla-Walla, now stained with the blood of God's servants, shed "like water round about," and the bloody work was not yet done. Mr. Kimball, with an arm broken, and otherwise badly wounded, remained in the chamber with the four sick children and the two oldest Sagar girls, Catherine and Elizabeth. They tore up a sheet, wound up his arm, and bandaged his bleeding body; but he suffered terribly all night, and became frantic for water in the morning; said he would have it if killed in the attempt. He crawled out to the river. A friendly Indian saw him and hid him in the brush, but, for reasons unknown, about sundown he crawled out and came toward his house. Catherine (who had come over with the children) says: "I heard the crack of a gun by my side and turned. Frank Escaloom, an Indian, was taking his gun from his face. Laughing, and pointing to the fence, he said: 'See how I make the Sugapoos (Americans) tumble.' Mr. Kimball was falling from the fence near the door, the blood running down the rails. Frank then stepped a little distance, took Susan Kimball by the arm, and laughingly said: 'See, I have killed your father, and you are to be my wife,' and dragged her away."

The same evening Mr. Young, coming down with a team, was met over the hill, a mile from the station, and shot. Two of the oxen were shot with him. The same afternoon, General Brouilette, Vicar-General for the Pope of Rome on this coast, arrived from the Umatilla at the camp of the murderers, which was close by the station, who kept up the scalp-dance all night, the screams of our helpless women, writhing in the hands of the unrestrained demons, in plain hearing.

But Wednesday a shocking deed was committed, that must shudder the heart of every American, and forever blacken and ruin the name of General Brouilette as a philanthropist, and cannot but equally blacken the characters of those persons in this country and in Washington, connected with the Government, who have taken pains to justify the savages and excuse Brouilette. He, the general, told me with his own lips, as the history will show: "This morning, after I baptized the children of the camp, I went over to see what I could do for the women and the dead bodies." Thus the new missionary, this priest of God, in the vestments of God, commenced his mission work in his new field, which he had emphatically gained by American blood, by baptizing those blood-stained children of these bloody savage murderers, the dead bodies yet lying unburied about him. For the last eighteen years I have not ceased to ask the unprejudiced what effect this baptizing in those circumstances had upon the minds of the Indians. There can but one answer be given. They understood the priest as approving what they had done and were doing. After the baptizing of the murderers, and after the bodies had been collected, sheets sewed around them by my daughter Eliza and others, and hauled by hand in wagons, put in a pit, and slightly covered, the Indians collected around the general, and insisted on his going to the doctor's medicines, to select out the poison, which it was said had been sent over by the fathers of Mrs. Whitman and Spaulding, and with which the doctor had been killing them, as he represented. Several depositions sustain this declaration.

Mr. McLane, secretary to Colonel Gilliam, says: "Soon after our forces left the garrison, we met a delegation from the Cayuse camp, headed by Stickus, who said: 'When we had but one religion, we had peace; but when another religion come, there was trouble. We were told the doctor was poisoning us; most of us didn't believe. But the Indians killed Dr. Whitman, and after he was dead the chief who told us these things came, and we told him to show us the poison. He went to the doctor's room, took up several little bottles, then selecting one and holding it said, 'This is the poison with which the doctor was killing you. Bury this in a box, or you will all be dead.'"

Miss Bewley, Catherine Sager, and Eliza Spaulding say that after the bodies were buried, the priest, who had been in the Indian camp over night, came into the large house where the captives were kept, and the Indians gathered around him and asked him to go to the doctor's medicines and find the poison. The priest went over to the doctor's house, and followed by multitudes of Indians, but by no white man except Joe Stanfield. "We trembled lest something should be found and made the pretense for killing us all. The Indian women were gathering around us with their dull tomahawks, and we expected every moment they would split our heads open. Joe Stanfield came out, the Indians following him, and said: ' The Father has found the poison; here it is;' holding up a phial which he put into a box with earth, nailed it up and took it away to bury it." And this Brouilette published a pamphlet in New York, in 1848, exculpating himself and associates, and filled it with just such falsehoods as we should expect; but, to our utter astonishment, ten years after, it is called for and printed by Congress, constituting Ex. Doc. No. 38, of Thirty-fifth Congress.

Sails and Bewley were removed to the large building and commenced to gain slowly. The helpless women and girls, bereft of their husbands, fathers, and brothers by the cruel tomahawk, stripped of their property, cattle, teams, their money, and even of their clothing till they had not enough to keep them from shivering, were subjected to a fate more terrific than death itself, and beyond the power of the pen to describe. The Indians admitted that in some cases they had to use the knife, their victims being so young. I am told by the volunteers that three Indians who reported these acts to them the next summer, rather boastingly, were missing the next day. Our captive women were compelled to cook for large numbers of the savages, every day, who would call upon Eliza to know if poison was put in their food, and requiring her to eat of it first. Robbed of most of her clothing, exposed to the cold and the smell of blood while sewing sheets around the offensive dead bodies, constant calls from the terrified white women and the Indians, to interpret for them, Eliza sunk down in a few days, and was laid almost helpless in the same room with Sails and Bewley. On the eighth day after the first butchery, three Indians came into the room and said that the great white chief at Umatilla had said that they must kill the two sick men to stop the dying of their people. (Hinman and Whitman testify the great chief was Bishop Blanchette.) They tore off the table-legs and commenced beating Sails and Bewley, and were full half an hour in killing them—their victims struggling over the floor and around the room, the blood and brains flying over my child, who was compelled to hear the blows and groans and witness the terrible scene. Miss Bewley attempted to rush in from another room, when she heard the agonies of her dying brother, but the women held her back. The bodies were thrown out at the door, and were not allowed to be buried for three days.

The next day, while the brother of Miss Bewley lay yet unburied at the door, my child Eliza, looking out of the door as she lay sick, and seeing an Indian ride up lead- a horse, cried out, "Oh there is Tashe—my horse; now I know the Indians have killed my father, for they have got my horse." The Indian came in, said he was sent to take that young woman, pointing to Miss Bewley, over to Umatilla, to be the wife of "Five Crows," a Cayuse chief. The horse he brought for her to ride was my own, and was Eliza's riding-horse, and recognized by her as soon as she saw it. This horse with three others, which I left in the hands of Brouilette when I met him and the Indian and fled for life, as the history will show, were found in his hands still, by the Nez Perces chiefs, James and Joseph, when I sent over for Eliza and the horses after I reached my home. So it seems that the horse that was sent to take Miss Bewley over to the Umatilla, to be subjected to the brutalities of the savage, was furnished by the vicar-general of the Jesuits on this coast, and the same agent who is now collecting unsuspecting young girls all through this great West, not for the same purposes, to be sure now, but for the large and flourishing schools throughout the country, of which he is the head.

But we let the amiable sufferer speak for herself. Her deposition was taken before Esquire Walling, then of Oregon City, 1848:

"After shaking with a chill of ague, and while the fever was yet raging and my head and bones in great pain, the Indian started with me for the Umatilla in the afternoon. I rode Eliza Spaulding's horse, which the Indian had brought for me. This led us to suppose that the Indians had killed Mr. Spaulding, somewhere. I had no choice, but had to submit to whatever the Indians directed. Although our fate as women and girls, in the hands of the savages who had murdered our husbands and fathers and brothers, was worse than death, still, when I took my fellow-sufferers by the hand to bid them farewell, the white women and children, my heart seemed ready to burst with grief. I fell upon the dead body of my dearest, dearest brother, yet unburied, and kissed his cold face all covered with his own blood. Oh that dear face that had ever been so precious to me, how could I leave it? I begged God to take my breath and let my cold body sleep by the side of his. The poor white women and children stood weeping very loud. Even the Indian women seemed moved. The Indians pulled me gently by the arm and pointed to the horse, and I was obliged to leave my dear brother lying cold and unburied, to see him no more. I was weeping so hard I could not see and could scarcely stand.

"The women and the Indians helped me along and helped me on the horse. Only the day before my brother was killed he told me he would soon be able to walk, and that he would leave in the night and find help to deliver us from our sufferings. I told him he was too sick yet, and besides, if he attempted such a thing, the Indians would kill him. He said he cared nothing for his life, if he could only deliver me from my sufferings. The Indians had abused me before his eyes, but he dared not raise his hand even if he had had the strength, and his groans of anguish on my account were harder, if possible, than my own. He had seen me dragged out by the savages and had become almost frantic, and declared he would try to deliver me if he died in the attempt. I had noticed Jo. Stanfield and Jo. Lewis listening to us, and think they overheard us, as word came from the Umatilla to kill my brother and Mr. Sails, and I have always felt the Catholics were the cause.

"The Indian led my horse, and as I rode away I thought my heart would burst with anguish. The idea of leaving my dear brother unburied; the idea of turning my back forever upon white people; to see my mother no more; to be doomed to suffer and live with the savages! Oh, how I begged God to send help or send death."

That night this amiable young saint lay down upon the prairies with but one blanket; the frozen earth, covered with snow, her night pillow; the dark heavens her curtains, her woes only growing darker and thicker at every step. No mother's hand or brother's to hold her aching head or stay the quivering flesh that seemed ready to fly off the bones, shaking so terribly with the cold and the ague. The Indian made a fire, which, however, lasted but a short time, and he was soon asleep in his single blanket. But what a night for that dear angel; it seemed a month, and yet she dreaded to have it end. The snow came down, and the chilling winds blew fiercely. "Has God and nature combined with the savages against me? No; I will not murmur. I will trust my God. He will do right for Jesus' sake." Yes; dear young sister, my fellow-sufferer to some extent, on those same cold, dark prairies, your Saviour, once in deeper agony, did hear your prayer, and was, even at that dark hour, working your and my deliverance by the only arm that could have been found west of the Rocky Mountains to have rescued us and our fellow-prisoners from a sure death or a perpetual captivity among the Indians.

Although the sufferings of that night were terrific and beyond the power of the pen, yet that dear girl could look forward to the dawn as the morning only of a day of fearful but accumulating woes. As soon as light dawned, without a moment's sleep, through the night from shivering cold, and without food, our dear victim, too cold or too weak to help herself, was helped on the horse, and they started. Thank God, it was Eliza's horse and very easy to ride. They reached Five Crows' lodge before noon. He went out and met her, and took her carefully in his arms from the horse, and led her into the lodge, spread down robes and blankets and laid her upon the bed, and built up a large fire and prepared two or three kinds of food and tea; but the terrible fever that followed the long chills, and the pains in her head and bones, would not allow her to eat. After she recovered so as to walk, the chief told her, if she wished, to go over to the house of the white men, (Bishop Blanchette and Brouilette,) and at night he would come for her. And she went over and went into the bishop's room. They had arrived at the Umatilla from Fort Walla-Walla two days before the massacre. And the company consisted of Bishop Blanchette, General Brouilette, two priests and three Frenchmen—seven white persons altogether. The three Frenchmen occupied the kitchen, and the other four the sitting-room or office, into which our helpless sister presented herself to the bishop and the priests, begging them that they would protect her and not allow the Indian to take her away. The darkness came, and with it the Indian, as she expected. He came into the kitchen near the middle door and spoke to Miss Bewley to come and go over home with him. He called to her several times, but she remained quiet and gave him no answer, and he soon turned away from the door and walked out, and then commenced a scene in that room that out-herods all that the bloody savages had done thus far, and here again we will let the helpless victim tell her own story:

"As soon as Five Crows left the door, Bishop Blanchette spoke first, and said: 'You had better go and be his wife.' I refused; I had rather die. Then Brouilette, who could speak better English, said, 'You must go, or he will come back and do us all an injury.' I arose, terrified at his words and looks, and commenced crying, begging him not to send me, and to have pity upon a poor, helpless girl. He said I must go, and he called to Joe, his servant, to take me over. And the servant came in. I fell upon my knees before the priest. 'Oh, do pity me—save me, save me; don't give me to the Indians, but shoot me.' He rose up and brushed away my hands, and said to the servant to take me over. I then sprang toward the two young priests, holding my hands appealingly, but they said nothing and moved not a hand, and the servant, half dragging, half carrying me, hurried me away. I can never describe the feelings of my soul as I cast a last look upon these white men."

The servant took her over to the Indian's lodge (half a mile distant,) opened the door, put her in, and turned back to the house. And now another scene opens in that lodge, most emphatically the counterpart of that blood-freezing scene I have related in the bishop's room. "As I was pushed into the lodge, the chief told me to sit down on a buffalo robe. A good fire was burning, and no one was in the lodge but the Indian. He was silent for some time, and then turned and said kindly to me, 'If you do not wish to be my wife, go back to the white man's house. I will not trouble you. Take your bundle of clothes.'" And she returned immediately to the bishop's house.

Well would it have been had our unfortunate daughter trusted to the humanity of the savage, rather than to the religion of the bishop. But instinctively the house of the white man was sought as soon as this frightened lamb found herself free from the hands of the dreadful Indians, and she found the bishop's house in the thick darkness, and sunk down on the floor in his room. And as they collected around her, she screamed and commenced begging them to save her, supposing she was to be again dragged away. But they soon quieted her by preparing a good bed and some food. The next day she begged them to send her to Fort Walla-Walla, for she feared the Indian would be persuaded to come again. She would work for them, or, should she live to reach the settlements, her friends would pay them any sum. The third day, at evening, just as she feared, the Indian came again, and stood at the same middle door and told her to come with him. And here again the former soul-sickening events were enacted over. But this time the Indian, having learned more of the designs of this spiritual adviser, remained to receive his victim. She says: "I was forced out of the room, and the Indian took me by the arm and led or dragged me away. And from that time I was subject to the Indian. I would return to the bishop every morning. One morning, as I was wringing my hands and crying, one of the young priests spoke kindly to me, telling me to pray to the Virgin. On another morning, as I came in, the other young priest laughingly asked me 'how I liked my new husband.' I thought this would break my heart, and cried through the day. About three weeks after the butchery, two Nez Perce chiefs, by the names of James and Red Wolf, came after Mr. Spalding's horses, which he had left with Brouilette, and brought us the news that Mr. Spalding had escaped and reached his family alive in the Nez Perce country, and that Mr. Canfield had also escaped and reached the same place. And what was to me most joyful news, they said efforts were being made to deliver all the captives. Although I could see no hope, the bare mention was a great comfort to my terrible situation.

"The next day, while the Nez Perces were yet there, word came that Mr. Ogden had arrived at Walla-Walla from Vancouver, with men, boats, and goods, to deliver the captives from the Indians, and that he had sent for the Cayuses and Walla-Wallas to come into council. Only those who have been in like fearful circumstances can have any idea of my frantic joy. I could not eat or sleep, or sit still, although the chills and the fever continued severe. I watched every motion of the trees, the birds, and the Indians, and every hour seemed a week. Three days after the first news of Mr. Ogden, Mr. Brouilette called to me in the morning to come out to him. He was on his horse to go to Walla-Walla. My heart leaped for joy with the hope that I was to be taken with him, but as I came up his look, as he pointed his finger, chilled my blood, and he said: 'Look here, if you go to that Indian's lodge to-night, stay there; don't come to my house again. Stay at one place or the other.'

"My blood curdled. In an instant I saw my fate was fixed, and not by the Indians; my breath almost stopped, and I only replied: 'But what can I do? The Indians will drag me away.' He replied: 'Remember what I tell you,' and put spurs to his mule, and was soon out of sight. I sank upon the ground almost senseless, and lay some time, but recovering a little, I begged God in mercy to take away my life. The chills returned as I lay upon the frozen ground, and it seemed as if the flesh would shake off my bones. The Indian would find me where I was, and I dreaded the house, but had to return to the bishop's room.

"The fever and the pains that followed were terrific, and yet the fearful forebodings for the future would make me forget these for a moment. I told one of the young priests what Brouilette had ordered, and begged him to protect me. He said the bishop did not like to have women about his house, but if the Indian came for me I would have to go. I asked if they would let me come back in the morning. He told me to come. When the Indian came in the evening, I tried to keep out of his way by going from one room to another, into the bishop's room, then into the kitchen among the men; he followed me, and tried to crowd me out of the door. He put my bonnet and shawl on. When his head was turned, I threw these under the bed and he did not find them, but he finally dragged me away without them.

"But thanks, everlasting thanks be to God, my deliverance came most unexpectedly. On the 28th of December, in the morning, while I was yet at the Five Crows' lodge, an Indian rode up leading a horse and handed me a note from Mr. Ogden, stating the joyful news that he had finally succeeded in redeeming all the unfortunate captives; that he had redeemed me. I had nothing to fear and nothing to do but to accompany the Indian as fast as I could, comfortably, to Walla-Walla. I could hardly believe my eyes. I bowed upon my knees with a grateful heart, and thanked my Saviour for his great mercy to me. The Five Crows prepared tea and a good breakfast for me, and put a new blanket and buffalo robe upon the saddle to make it comfortable for me to ride and for sleeping at night, and a thick shawl around me, and assisted me on my horse, and bade me goodbye kindly and with much feeling, and gave me food for the journey. Again I was riding with a lone Indian over the prairies, but with very different feelings from those of three weeks before. Indeed, I cannot describe my feelings. My joy was unspeakable, and yet I might be seized by the hands that had deceived me in the hour of greatest peril. Although I was more fit for the sick-bed than a journey on horseback of 55 miles in the winter, yet I found myself urging the horse sometimes upon the lope. It was a gentle and easy-going horse. The night was cold, with a thick fog. The Indian found a good camping place on the Walla-Walla, and soon had a good fire, and replenished it several times through the night, seemingly for my benefit. Although I had bedding enough, and the good fire to keep me comfortable, my joy kept me from sleep. At dawn the Indian was up, built a rousing fire, and brought in the horses which he had hobbled out, and took great pains to prepare my breakfast, with tea in a cup he had with him, and then after he worshipped, in which I joined most heartily, although I understood but a few of his words, he saddled my horse and arranged my robe and blanket and helped me on, and we rode off; and when we came in sight of the fort, the Indian pointed it out to me, and said, 'House,' 'suyapu aiat'—American woman. I thought my heart would jump out of my bosom.

"As we rode up, Governor Ogden and Mr. McBean, with several Catholic priests and half-breed women, came out. Mr. Ogden took me gently from the horse, as a father, and said, 'Thank God, I have got you safe at last. I had to pay the Indians more for you than for all the other captives, and I feared they would never give you up.' Mr. McBean provided a good bed for me, and treated me very kindly. They took me into Mr. Osborne's room, where I found Mrs. Osborne very sick, and her hip bones cut through the skin on the floor. All the captives from Walleiptu were brought in that night. Two days after, Mr. Spalding and family, and Mr. Craig and Canfield, were brought in by the Nez Perces.

"LORINDA BEWLEY.

Subscribed and sworn to before me, this 12th day of December, 1848, at Oregon City, Oregon Territory.

G. WALLING,
Justice of the Peace.

Deposition of John Kimzey.

On my way to this country, with my family, last fall, I called at Fort Walla-Walla to exchange my teams and wagon for horses.

There were at the fort two Roman Catholic priests.

During my stay of about two days, Mr. McBean, in the presence of my wife, said the fathers had offered to purchase Dr. Whitman's station, but Dr. Whitman had refused to sell. He said they had requested the doctor to fix his own price, and they would meet it, but the doctor had refused to sell on any conditions. I asked him who he meant by the fathers; he said the holy fathers, the Catholic priests. He said the holy fathers were about to commence a mission at the mouth of the Utilla, one in the upper part of the Utilla, one near Dr. Whitman's station, if they could not get hold of the station, one in several other places which I can not name.

They hired Mr. Marsh, whose tools I brought, to do off a room for the priests at the fort.

He said Dr. Whitman had better leave the country immediately, or the Indians will kill him; we are determined to have his staiion.

He further said, I think Mr. Spalding will also have to leave the country soon.

As I was about leaving, Mr. McBean said, if you could pass as an Englishman, the Indians would not injure you; if they do disturb you, show them the horses and the mark, and they will know my horses; show them by signs that you are from the fort, and they will let you pass. The Indians noticed the mark on the horses, and did not disturb me.

JOHN KIMZEY.

Subscribed and sworn to before me, at my office in Tualatin Plains, Tualatin County, this 28th day of August, 1848.

DAVID T. LENOX,
Justice of the Peace.

It is a fact that should be made known to the American people, that while the Catholic missionaries in Oregon were thus baptizing the children of the murdering savages while they were butchering American fathers and brothers, were tearing our escaped fathers out of their houses, and refusing admittance to our escaped American mothers and infants, and handling our helpless young women to the savages to be the sport of their atrocities, and furnishing the savages war material to destroy the American settlements on the Pacific shores, our American missionary, Dr. Parker, was furnishing protection and safety under the American flag, at his own house in China, to Catholic priests, to save them from death at the hands of the exasperated Chinese, and with his own Protestant hands smoothed the dying pillow of one of them who expired soon after he got him to his house. (See Dr. Parker's report as United States minister to China in the documents at Washington.)

Testimony of Miss Bewley.

Questions to Miss Bewley: When did the priest arrive?—Answer. Wednesday, while the bodies were being prepared for the grave. The bodies were collected into the boxes on Tuesday evening.

Q. Did the Indians bury a vial or bottle of the doctor's medicine?—A. They said they did. Jo. Stanfield made the box to bury it in, and the Indians said they buried it.

Q. Why did they bury it?—A. They said the priests said it was poison. Stanfield and Nichols were their interpreters to us.

Q. How did they obtain this vial?—A. The Indians said the priest found it among the doctor's medicine, and showed it to them, and told them if it broke it would poison the whole nation.

Q. Was there much stir among the Indians about this vial?—A. Yes, a great deal.

Q. Why did the Indians kill your brother?—A. Edward Telankaikt (chief's son) returned from the Umatilla, and told us (after they had killed him) the great chief had told them their disease would spread.

(It will be seen by Hinman's deposition, and by J. B. Whitman's, that by the great chief is meant the principal white man at a given place, and that Bishop Blanchette was the principal white at Umatilla, at this time.)

Q. Did the Indians threaten you all and treat you with cruelty from the first, and threaten your lives on Tuesday, the day the priest was there?—A. Yes, and frequently threatened our lives afterward.

Q. When were you taken to the Umatilla?—A. Just at night on Tuesday, December 7, the next week after the first massacre, having shaken with the ague that day; slept out that night in the snow storm.

Q. Whose horses came for you?—A. Eliza Spalding said they belonged to her father; this led us to suppose that Mr. Spalding was killed.

Q. When did you leave Umatilla?—A. On Monday, (December 27,) before the Saturday (January 1, 1848) on which Mr. Spalding and company arrived, and we all started the next day for the lower country.

Q. Did you learn that the priests made arrangements to commence missions at Dr. Whitman's and Mr. Spalding's?—A. When at Umatilla the Frenchman told me that they were making arrangements to locate the priests; two at Mr. Spalding's, as soon as Mr. Spalding got away, and two at the doctor's, and they were going to the doctor's next week to build a house.

Q. Did Dr. Whitman wish to have Jo. Lewis stop at his place?—A. He let him stop only because he said he had no shoes nor clothes and could not go on. The doctor furnished Jo. with shoes and shirts; and got him to drive a team, but he was gone but three days and returned; but the doctor did not like it. I heard Mrs. Whitman say Jo. was making disturbance among the Indians. I heard the doctor say once, "Now we shall have trouble, these priests are coming; I think the Indians have given them land." Mrs. Whitman said, "It will be a wonder if they do not come and kill us."

Testimony of Dr. Saffrons.

JESUITS AND HUDSON'S BAY MEN MAKE SAVAGES BELIEVE DR. WHITMAN TO BE A DANGEROUS MAN—FORT WALLA-WALLA INTENDED THE AMERICAN FAMILIES AT DALLES SHOULD BE KILLED.

Question. Where were you when you heard of the massacre, and how did you know it?—Answer. I was stopping at Dalles mission. Mr. and Mrs. Hinman and P. B. Whitman, nephew of Dr. Whitman, missionaries, and William McKinney and wife, emigrants, stopping to winter, constituted the whites. A Frenchman, as express from Walla-Walla to Vancouver, had arrived in haste, and desired Mr. Hinman to assist him on as all the men at the Fort Walla-Walla had died of measles, and Mr. Hinman had left for Vancouver. Scarcely had they gone when the Indians came in and told us that Dr. Whitman and wife, and all the Americans at his station, had been killed by the Cayuse; that the Frenchman had told them so. We could not believe it, as no letter had arrived from Walla-Walla, and the Frenchman had told us that he did not believe that Dr. W. was dead. Some days after an Indian came and said the Cayuse had collected at Des Chutes; that they said the Catholic priests had made known to them that the doctor was a dangerous medicine-man to have among them; that Mr. McBean, in charge of Fort Walla-Walla, had said that Dr. Whitman determined to have all their spotted horses.

HENRY SAFRONS.

Subscribed and sworn to before me this 9th day of February, 1849, at Oregon City, Oregon Territory.

GABRIEL WALLING,
Justice of the Peace.

Bishop Blanchette's letter to Governor Abernathy.

HIS DUPLICITY AND DIRECT FALSEHOOD TO DECEIVE THE WORLD AS TO HIS AND BROUILETTE'S CRIME TO MISS BEWLEY.

UMATILLA, *December* 21, 1847.

PLEASE YOUR EXCELLENCY: The Indians, in a moment of despair, have committed acts of atrocity. They have murdered Dr. Whitman, his wife, and the Americans who lived with him. Mr. Brouilette, vicar-general of Walla-Walla, arrived at Waiilatpu on Tuesday evening, and therefore the first time heard the painful intelligence. As soon as I had been informed of what had happened, I instantly sent for the chiefs, ("Five Crows," the chief to whom they had given Miss Bewley, was one,) whose lodges are near my house. After having made known to them without delay how much I was grieved in consequence of the commission of such an atrocious act, I told them I hoped the women and children would be spared till they could be sent to the Willamette. They answered, "We pity them; they shall not be harmed; they shall be taken care of as before." I have since had the satisfaction to learn they have been true to their word, and they have taken care of these poor people. [It will be seen by Miss Bewley's deposition that this ever-to-be-pitied, amiable young woman was at this time in that bishop's house and had been there from the 9th and continued till the 27th, forced out by the bishop himself into the Indian's lodge, who did not, however, at first abuse her, but sent her back to the bishop's house, one-half a mile; but the third night, being forced out, the Indian dragged her away; returning in the morning, she was forced out every night. She says the Indian would drag me away. She said to Catharine Geiger she would hold on to the table till she pulled the skin from her fingers. And yet the bishop, during this time, on 21st, six days before she is delivered, says to Governor Abernathy, "They have taken care of these poor people." Here is a direct falsehood, and to cover up the most brutal crime upon a helpless young woman ever committed. The rest of the letter shows who had control over the Indians to make war or peace.] I was enabled to make new efforts not only to save the women and children, but also the Rev. H. H. Spalding and his family, and the Americans at his station, [after the chief he had designated to kill me had declined and the party he sent there to butcher Mrs. Spalding and brother had been defeated by the Nez Perces.] That the tragedy of the 29th had occurred from an anxious desire of self-defense; that it was the report made against the doctor that led them to commit this act. Your excellency will have to judge of the value of this document, [purporting to be the speeches of the Cayuse chiefs, but manifestly made up by the priests,] which I have the honor to forward to you by request. Nevertheless, without having the least intention to influence you one way or the other, I feel myself obliged to tell you that by going to war with the Cayuses you will have, undoubtedly, all the Indians of this country against you. Would it be to the interest of a young colony to expose herself? But that you will have to decide.

Receive the assurance of the highest consideration with which I am your excellency's very humble and most obedient servant,

BLANCHETTE,
Bishop of Walla Walla.

His Excellency GEORGE ABERNATHY,
Governor of Territory of Oregon.

Depositions of Wilcox, Marsh, and Hinman.

The night after Mr. Kimzey left the fort, he overtook me at the mouth of the Utilla, and camped with me. He appeared much concerned about what he had learned at the fort. He told me much about what Mr. McBean said about the Catholic priests trying to buy the Doctor's station. Among other things, I remember Mr. Kimsey said, that Mr. McBean said, that if the Doctor does not leave the Indians will kill him, and, says Mr. Kimsey, I believe they will. I remarked, the Catholics have not got that station yet.

F. S. WILCOX.

Sworn to and subscribed before me, at my office in Tualatin Plains, Tualatin County, the 28th day of August, 1848.

DAVID T. LENOX,
Justice of the Peace.

These men moved on with the emigration of that fall, but before they reached the Willamette, the news of the Waiilatpu tragedy overtook them.

Mr. Marsh, son of the Mr. Marsh who was killed, testifies as follows: "I left my father and little sister at Dr. Whitman's mission two weeks before the massacre, and went down to Walla Walla and got work, and, while there, I heard Mr. McBean say in the presence of the priest, 'Doctor Whitman and Mr. Spalding had better leave or the Indians will kill them, for the fathers will have those stations.'"

LUCIUS MARSH.

Sworn to and submitted before me at my office in Tualatin Plains, Tualatin County, this 28th day of August, 1848.

DAVID T. LENOX,
Justice of the Peace.

Mr. Hinman, who had charge of our mission station at the Dalles, with Perri Whitman, nephew of Doctor Whitman, as interpreter, testifies: "On the 3d of December, 1847, after breakfast, the Indians came in and said a Frenchman was down at the river. I told them to call him up. He came and sat down to breakfast. I asked, 'What news from above?' 'All the men are dead at Walla-Walla except Mr. McBean and myself, and I am in a great hurry to get to Vancouver, to have other men come up. Can you help me to a canoe and Indians? Mr. McBean wished you would.' 'What killed them?' 'The measles.' 'Have you heard from Dr. Whitman?' 'Yes; I heard he was dead.' 'When?' 'Four weeks ago; but I don't believe it.' 'Well, I have to go down to Vancouver, and will go down now.' And as soon as I could get ready we started, in my canoe, with Indians. But on reaching Cape Horn the wind stopped us, and I made a camp and lay down; but I noticed the Frenchman was much agitated; he would walk up and down the river, and come and look earnestly at me, and go away, and come back again. Finally he came up, and fixing his eyes upon me exclaimed, 'Very bad man, me, Mr. Hinman. Big lie I tell you—no man dead at Walla-Walla; but Dr. Whitman be dead; all the Americans at Doctor's dead; Indians have killed them; I see them with my eyes, the day before I start; I see Mrs. Whitman dead; Indians got all women and children prisoners. I take letter to Vancouver for the company to come quick and get all American women and children before Indian he kill them.' Mr. Hinman said, 'Why did you not tell me at home? Now the Indians have probably come down and killed my family.' 'Very bad man, Mr. Hinman; but the priests tell me not to tell you and Americans at Dalles. If I tell you they no pardon my sins; but I have to tell you; too much terror here'—putting his hand to his breast. Mr. Hinman knew not whether to turn back to save his family, or to push ahead to give the company the news and the opportunity to send up the sooner; but he pushed on, reached Vancouver, went into Mr. Ogden's office, and delivered the letters and reported the awful news. 'Just what I expected,' said Mr. Ogden, 'when those eight priests went up a few weeks ago.' The letters being directed to Mr. Douglass, they all walked into his office, and, throwing down the letters, Mr. Ogden said, 'There, see what a war in religion has done. The good doctor is dead. I knew there would be trouble when those priests went up.' 'Tut, tut, Mr. Ogden, don't be too hasty,' said Mr. Douglass, and opened the letters and read: 'Dr. Whitman is killed; Mrs. Whitman is killed; Indians are after Spalding, &c., &c., and moreover parties are fitting out; one to go to the mill, one to go to the Spokane mission to kill all at those stations; and to go to Clear Water; and one to g—my God, Hinman, why are you here?—to the Dalles.'" "Sure enough," said Mr. Hinman. "Why was that Frenchman forbid to tell me; and I only heard of it just up here at Cape Horn." The tables were now turned upon Mr. Douglass, who replied: "You must remember that man was in trying circumstances." Mr. Douglass transcribed that letter to Governor Abernathy for the "Oregon Spectator," but that sentence was left out, and but for Mr. Hinman's providential presence the world would not have known that the man who was bearing a letter by the Dalles, containing a declaration that a party of savage murderers was to start to kill the families at that place, was forbidden to warn them of their danger on pain of not having his sins pardoned; and when asked by Mr. Hinman about the doctor, said he did not believe he was dead, but he was the man sent out to look for horses, attracted by a crowd about the doctor's, who rode there on Tuesday and saw the dead bodies lying about; saw the doctor's body and Mrs. Whitman's and returned to Walla-Walla that evening and started the next morning for Vancouver with the letters. P. B. Whitman says, in his deposition before Esquire Purdy, of Salem: "About twenty minutes after Mr. Hinman and the Frenchman had left for Vancouver, a crowd of Indians came into the room and sat down silently for some time, and then exclaimed, "Why are you not crying?" "Why?" "Because your father and mother are dead; all the Americans are dead; the Cayuse have killed them." "How do you know?" "The Frenchmen told us that he saw them lying dead about the doctor's house just before he started; and he has gone to Husushuihai (Whitehead's Vancouver) for them to send up men and goods to purchase the many captive women and children." "That can not be," I replied; "the Frenchman told us that he had not seen the doctor, my uncle, for two weeks, and did not believe he was dead; but that all the men at the fort except himself and Mr. McBean were dead; that he was going to Vancouver for more men to man the post. Besides, we have received no letters from Walla-Walla; but if my uncle and the Americans at his place had been killed, we surely would have received letters from Mr. McBean or the priests." There were six Americans at the Dalles, viz: Mr. and Mrs. Hinman (missionaries), Mr. and

Mrs. McKinney, (emigrants,) P. B. Whitman, and Doctor Saffrons. As they had received no intimation from the Frenchman, who was direct from Walla-Walla, and had received no letters from that post, which they certainly would, had the doctor and the emigrants been killed, as represented by the Indians, they could not believe for a moment the report of the Indians. But still the Indians about the station became more and more excited from day to day, and finally took their women and effects to the mountains; and the day before Mr. Hinman's return, several painted, naked Cayuse showed themselves in the vicinity of the station.

It is a question of vital importance to American Protestants, not of that day only, but of the present day, why that Frenchman was ordered not to let Americans at the Dalles know their danger; why he was threatened with that most fearful of all punishments, more than fines or imprisonment, to deter him from telling them. Why did not Mr. McBean or the priests write by that messenger to the Dalles, when they knew a party of the murderers was soon to start to kill them? Why was the Frenchman told to obtain Mr. Hinman to go on with him, if possible, thus leaving his family more exposed?

Questions to Mr. Hinman: Did you ever hear Dr. Whitman express fears concerning influence which Catholics were exerting among the Indians?

Hinman's answer: I have heard him say several times that he had no fears but that the mission would prosper only from the Catholic influence.

Q. Do you know anything of the *Catholic ladder?*—A. I saw one in the hands of the Indians at the Dalles, and heard them speak of others. The object of this painting was to represent Protestants leading Indians to hell, and Catholics leading Indians to heaven.

Q. Did you ever hear the Indians say they had been told by Catholics and Frenchmen that American missionaries were causing them to die?—A. Yes, very often.

Q. Who would you understand by the term "great chief," as used by the Indians?—A. The principal white man among them.

Q. Who was the principal white man at Umatilla at the time of Whitman's massacre?—A. Bishop Blanchette.

Q. How did Dr. Whitman regard the Cayuse as to their readiness to receive instructions?—A. The last time I saw him, which was a few weeks before the butchery, he was greatly encouraged.

Q. Did the Frenchman tell you that he saw the dead bodies of Dr. and Mrs. Whitman?—A. He said he was out on Tuesday looking after the horses of the post; saw a great multitude of the Indians about the doctor's house; rode there; saw the bodies of Dr. and Mrs. Whitman and others lying about. The Indians told him to alight and not be afraid. He saw the doctor and John lying in the house; Mrs. Whitman, Mr. Rodgers and Francis lying in the mud near the kitchen door; others at a little distance. Crows were upon them; they were badly cut to pieces.

ALANSON HINMAN.

Subscribed and sworn to before me this 9th day of April, 1849.

JOST J. HEMBREE,
Justice of the Peace in and for the county of Yamhill, O. T.

AMERICAN CONGRESS vs. PROTESTANTISM IN OREGON.

WITNESS FOR THE DEFENSE, NO. 2—WHAT THE PEOPLE OF OREGON AND WASHINGTON THINK OF EXECUTIVE DOCUMENT NO. 38.

To the honorable the Senate and House of Representatives of the Congress of the United States:

The memorial of the undersigned, Henry H. Spalding, of the State of Oregon, late missionary of the American Board of Commissioners of Foreign Missions to the Indians, in the former Territory of Oregon, respectfully represents:

That Marcus Whitman, M. D., a citizen of the United States, and a native of the State of New York, did, in 1836, by official permit from the War Department of the United States, proceed to the Pacific shores, then almost wholly unknown to our people and totally unappreciated, and ostensibly in the joint occupancy of the United States and Great Britain, but really under the exclusive control of the Hudson's Bay Company, a British monopoly, governed by a board of directors in London, with 55 sworn officers in the Territory, and 515 articled men, and over 800 half-breeds and all the Indian tribes under their control, with a line of well-established and strongly fortified posts extending from the Pacific to the Atlantic shores, and having complete control of the Pacific coast for over 2,000 miles, deriving a yearly revenue of over $40,000, and who had succeeded by their power and the aid of the savages in forcing the last American trader from the country.

And that said Dr. Whitman, by order of the American Board of Commissioners for Foreign Missions, established an American mission in the valley of the Walla-Walla, in said Territory of Oregon, and by his travels as missionary made himself acquainted with the value of the country, both for settlement and for its mineral wealth; and having demonstrated the problem that wagons and families could cross the mountains and the continent by bringing his wagons through in 1836.

And that said Whitman, by his sleepless vigilance, became convinced that a deep-laid plan was about culminating to secure this rich country of Oregon Territory to Great Britain from misrepresentations on the part of Great Britain and for want of information as to the character and value of the country on the part of the Government of the United States.

And that to prevent the sale and transfer of said Territory, and the consequent loss to the United States of this great Northwest and its valuable seaboard, and the great commercial considerations therewith, said Whitman did, in the dead of winter, at his own expense, and without asking or expecting a dollar from any source, cross the continent, amid the snows of the Rocky Mountains and the bleakness of the intervening plains, inhabited by hostile savages, suffering severe hardships and perils from being compelled to swim broad, rapid, and ice-floating rivers, and to wander lost in the terrific snow-storms, subsisting on mule and dog meat, and reached the city of Washington not an hour too soon, confronting the British agents Ashburton, Fox, and Simpson, who, there is evidence to show, in a short time would have consummated their plans, and secured a part, if not all, of our territory west of the mountains to Great Britain, and by his own personal knowledge disproving their allegations, and by communicating to President Tyler important information concerning the country, and the fact that he had taken his wagons and mission families through years before, and that he proposed taking back a wagon-train of emigrants that season, did thereby prevent the sale and loss of this our rich Pacific domain to the people of the United States.

And that said Whitman did then return to Oregon Territory and conduct the first wagon-train of 1,000 souls to the Columbia River, thereby greatly increasing American influence, and completely breaking the influence of the British monopoly and adding immensely to the courage and wealth of the little American settlement, and continued, at his mission station in the Walla-Walla Valley, to furnish needed supplies to the yearly emigrants, and a resort for them to rest and recruit, until he and his heroic wife and her equally heroic associate, Mrs. Spalding, together with seventeen other emigrants who had stopped to winter, were brutally destroyed in 1847 by the Indians, and the American settlements in Middle Oregon broken up, and a bloody war to exterminate the Americans on the Pacific coast commenced.

And that there is abundant proof to show that the said Whitman massacre, and the long and expensive wars that followed, were commenced by the above-said British monopoly for the purpose of breaking up the American settlements and of regaining the territory, and that they were especially chagrined against the said Whitman as being the principal agent in disappointing their schemes.

And said proof consists in—

1. A pamphlet published by an agent from Europe, connected with the Hudson's Bay Company, who was on the ground during the bloody tragedy, and walked unharmed amid the slaughter, which lasted eight days, encouraging the savages, in which he says, "The massacre of Waiilatpu has not been committed by the Indians in hatred of the heretics. If Americans only have been killed, it is because the war has been declared by the Indians against the Americans only, and not against foreigners; and it was in their quality as American citizens and not as Protestants that the Indians killed them."

2. The said agent, with his associates and officers of the Hudson's Bay Company, turned out the escaped Americans from their posts, one of whom was murdered by the Indians, and they also refused admittance to mothers and their infants during the slaughter, and with their own hands, for fifteen nights, handed one of our American girls to the savages, to be the sport of their atrocities.

3. One of the overland companions of this agent, from Canada, gave the signal for the tomahawk to commence, and shot Mrs. Whitman with his own hand.

4. Defying the infant provisional government, and remaining in the hostile country furnishing our enemies with war material after that country was closed against all whites.

5. Attempting to furnish the combined hostiles from the English post, at Fort Vancouver, in the Hudson's Bay Company's boats, with Hudson's Bay men in charge of one of their agents, with over four thousand pounds of powder and ball, and three cases of guns, which were taken from them at Fort Wascopum by Lieutenant Rogers, only fifteen miles short of the hostile camp, waiting at the river Des Chutes, who boasted three days before that such ammunition was coming up by such agents to them, and that when they obtained it they would fall upon the American settlements and destroy them, and take their women and cattle and herds.

6. The sudden building of fortifications at Fort Vancouver.

7. The significant boast of Sir George Simpson, only a few months before this bloody work commenced, published in his Voyage Around the World, viz: "I defy the American Congress to establish their Atlantic tariff in the Pacific ports."

It is not, therefore, too much to say that Dr. Marcus Whitman and those heroic women lost their lives in consequence of their services aforesaid, which they so heroically and lavishly gave to their country and a pure Christianity.

And that a document has been published by order of Congress, entitled Executive Document No. 38, of the Thirty-fifth Congress, (doubtless through one of those inadvertencies which sometimes occur in the proceedings of deliberative bodies,) which document casts severe reflections upon the memory of said Dr. Whitman and his compatriots, as also upon the early Protestant missions in Oregon, attempting to show that they rendered no benefit to the country, but "set a bad example to the races among whom they chose to dwell," and were the real causes of the massacre and of the war.

In connection with this memorial, the undersigned respectfully invites attention to the following documents bearing on the case, viz:

Document A. Memorial to Governor Ballard, signed by E. R. Geary, and some 700 citizens of Oregon, and Elwood Evans and others, of Washington Territory.

Document B. Resolutions of the Presbyterian Church, (Old School,) signed by A. L. Lindsley, moderator, and E. R. Geary, stated clerk.

Document C. Resolutions of the Oregon Presbytery of the Cumberland Presbyterian Church, W. R. Bishop, moderator; C. Wooley, stated clerk.

Document D. Resolutions of Oregon United Presbyterian Church, Jeremiah Dick, moderator; T. S. Kendal, stated clerk.

Document E. Resolutions of the Oregon Association of the Congregational Church, G. H. Atkinson, moderator; C. N. Terry, clerk.

Document F. Resolutions of the Oregon Conference, Methodist Episcopal Church, Bishop Kingsley, moderator; C. C. Stratton, clerk.

Document G. Resolutions of the Pleasant Bute Baptist Church, State of Oregon, J. W. Warmouth, moderator; H. J. C. Averill, clerk.

Document H. Resolutions of the Oregon Brotherhood of the Christian Church, J. M. Harris, moderator; W. H. Rowland, clerk.

Document I. Resolutions of the Steuben Presbytery, Presbyterian Church, New York, D. Henry Palmer, J. H. Hotchkiss, O. F. Marshall, committee.

Document J. Memorial of the citizens of Steuben County, Alleghany County, and Chemung County, New York. Signed by O. F. Marshall, George Edwards, J. W. Hoffman, and others.

Document K. Memorial of the citizens of Oberlin, Ohio, signed by President Fairchild, and others.

Now, therefore, in view of the great wrong and injustice done to the cause of Protestant missions, on the ground, to the memory of martyrs whose services there were of so signal advantage to the country as such, as well as to the cause of religion, and the undersigned personally, the present Congress is respectfully and earnestly petitioned so far to review the action of the Twenty-fifth Congress, as to issue, in documentary form, a suitable vindication of the parties mentioned. Your honorable body is respectfully but earnestly requested to publish, in a like Congressional document, the reply or manifesto herewith transmitted.

And your memorialist feels the utmost assurance that the sacred regard for the truth of history ever entertained, and the high value ever placed upon unselfish patriotism by your honorable body, will lead you at once to see both the justice and the patriotism of his humble prayer.

HENRY H. SPALDING,
Of Oregon.

We hope Congress will appoint a committee of investigation, and if faithful and patriotic men and women have been publicly wronged, let them be righted as publicly before the nation.—New York Observer, October, 1867.

Official slander of martyred missionaries attempted.—Dayton (Ohio) Telescope, January, 1870.

PHELPS, DODGE & CO.,
(Cliff street, between John and Fulton,)
New York, December 29, 1870.

MY DEAR SIR: This will introduce the Rev. H. H. Spalding, long a missionary of the American Board of Commissioners for Foreign Missions in Oregon, who visits Washington by the advice of many friends to see if the great wrong done to the memory of his companion in the mission, Rev. Dr. Whitman, cannot be rectified by Congress.

I have known of the facts for many years, and the inclosed, if you can take time to look them over, will deeply interest you, and show you how our Government has, no doubt ignorantly, done great injustice to one who deserved the highest commendation for what he had done for the nation.

I beg you to take a little time in looking into this matter, and consulting with other friends of Protestant religion, to see if we cannot wipe out this stain.

Very respectfully, yours,

W. E. DODGE.

Hon. JAMES G. BLAINE,
Speaker United States House of Representatives, Washington, D. C.

PHILADELPHIA, January 5, 1871.

I fully concur in the sentiments and wishes of Hon. W. E. Dodge.

JAY COOKE.

A like circular was addressed by the eminent patriots to Senators Colfax, Patterson, Pomeroy, Buckingham, and Wilson; to Cattell, Armstrong, and Maynard, of the House of Representatives.

OFFICE OF THE OREGON CENTRAL RAILROAD COMPANY,
Salem, November 8, 1869.

DEAR SIR: Your favor of 29th ultimo came duly to hand per last mail; contents noted. I assure you I will gladly do what I can to aid in rendering justice to those noble-minded men and women, (martyrs to truth and a pure Christianity,) which our too lenient, and in this instance criminally careless, Government permitted itself to abuse in such unscrupulous manner as was done by the publication, authoritatively, of Ex. Doc. 38, referred to in yours.

Very truly, yours,

J. R. MOORES.

JAMES BLAKELY, Esq.,
Chairman of Committee.

DOCUMENT K.

Whereas the United States Congress published in Executive Document No. 38, 1859, an ex parte statement of what is known as the Whitman massacre, and of the causes that led to it, which reflects severely upon the devoted missionaries of the American Board then laboring on the Pacific shores, and does great injustice to those faithful martyrs to a pure Christianity:

Therefore resolved, That we, citizens of Oberlin, unite with the thousands of patriotic brethren on the Pacific slopes in respectfully and earnestly petitioning Congress to take the steps requisite to correct the wrong to the memory of the patriotic dead, and extend justice to the living.

JAS. H. FAIRCHILD,
President.
JOHN M. ELLIS,
Professor of Intellectual Philosophy.
JUDSON SMITH,
Professor of Ecclesiastical History.
C. H. CHURCHILL,
Professor of Mathematics.
G. W. STEELE,
Professor of Music.
S. F. PORTER,
Congregational Minister.
R. THEO. CROSS,
Principal of Preparatory Department.
G. W. SHURTLEFF,
Professor of Latin.
DUDLEY ALLEN, M. D.
JOHN MORGAN,
Professor of Biblical Literature.
D. P. REAMER.
HIRAM HULBURD.
E. J. GOODRICH.
J. T. SIDDALL.

Whereas we, citizens of Almond, N. Y., having listened with great interest for two evenings to the statements of the Rev. H. H. Spalding, relative to his missionary journey, in company with Dr. M. Whitman, his own and the doctor's heroic wife, across the Rocky Mountains in 1836, the establishment of a mission among the Nez Perces Indians; the success attending their efforts in reducing the language to writing; in establishing schools and churches; and in introducing among that tribe many of the arts and comforts of civilization; the uncompensated labors of Dr. Whitman in encountering the perils of the journey in mid-winter across the continent to Washington, and making such representations to the Government as to secure to the United States the States and Territories on the Pacific Coast; the bloody drama by which the mission was broken up—the barbarous savages being spurred on by the willful lies of Catholic emissaries; and the passage by the Thirty-fifth Congress of Ex. Doc. No. 38, by which the missionaries of the American Board of Commissioners for Foreign Missions were driven from the field, and have never been permitted to return; and whereas all these allegations are supported by documentary evidence and unimpeachable testimony: Therefore,

1. *Resolved*, That we see the wonder-working hand of Providence in thus opening the way for the establishment of a mission among the Indian tribes beyond the Rocky Mountains, and the raising up and qualifying missionaries, like Dr. Whitman and Rev. Mr. Spalding, and their Christian wives, for this work.

2. That in our judgment a grievous wrong has been done Dr. Whitman and his martyred associates, in the passage by the Thirty-fifth Congress of Ex. Doc. No. 38; and that, in common with our patriotic fellow-citizens of the Pacific coast, we unite in asking Congress to rectify this wrong, in part, at least, by adopting and publishing a document which shall contain an answer to the above-named document; and we feel the utmost assurance that the sacred regard for the truth of history ever entertained by your honorable body, and the high name ever placed by you upon unselfish patriotism, will lead you at once to see both the justice and patriotism of our request.

E. W. EWERS.	A. SPRAGUE.
M. M. HENRY.	H. W. CRANDALL.
THEO. H. RUEDIGER.	JONAS G. PRENTISS.
JAMES GOODRICH.	WM. RICHARDSON.
C. S. HALL.	CASS RICHARDSON.
IRA CUTLER.	ISAAC G. OGDEN.
C. CURTIS.	

MANIFESTO: OR A REPLY TO EXECUTIVE DOCUMENT NO. 38 OF THE THIRTY-FIFTH CONGRESS.

NEWBURYPORT, MASS., *January* 6, 1871.

REV. AND DEAR SIR: Your continued life and your return to the Atlantic slope call for renewed gratitude from Christian hearts. * * * * *

We give thanks for your existence, for what God has wrought in you and done by you; and even more than in former years we glorify God in you.

Our nation owes you a debt it can never pay. Our American Israel—the members of Christ's body, in our land—are under obligations to you that may be understood better in Heaven than on earth. The pioneer missionaries on the Pacific slope are to be honored forever for being such faithful servants of Zion's King, whose kingdom shall stand forever. How great the blessing to be called of God and to be girded for the work of laying the foundation for many generations. Saved by the blood and righteousness of Christ, you will soon unite with the spirits of the just made perfect in praising God for what He has wrought through human agency in our world, and you will know the bliss of enduring gratitude for what, by His grace, He has aided you to accomplish for the advancement of His kingdom.

Your sister in Christ,

Z. B. BANISTER.

Mr. H. H. SPALDING.

[From the Elmira (N. Y.) Herald, December 5, 1870.]

A REMARKABLE VISITOR.

The Rev. Henry H. Spalding, on his way to Washington from Oregon, is to spend to-day or to-morrow in this city, and will address the people in one or more of the churches. His history is one of striking interest. With the Rev. Marcus Whitman, he undertook a mission to the Indians of Oregon as long ago as 1836. Their wives were the first white women who crossed the Rocky Mountains, and thus made it evident that families could traverse the plains to the Pacific coast. Dr. Whitman afterwards returned on horseback, in mid-winter, to communicate with Daniel Webster, then Secretary of State, and in treaty with Great Britain for the northwest territory, and demonstrated to him and President Tyler the accessibility and desirableness of that country to our Republic, so that this missionary company may be credited with securing that vast and valuable portion of our country to this Government, instead of suffering it to fall under British rule.

In 1847 a terrible uprising of Indians occurred, resulting in breaking up all American settlements in Eastern Oregon, and the massacre of nearly the entire missionary band, who had there labored for eleven years in their self-denying enterprise.

Mr. Spalding is the only survivor of the band, his wife having perished in consequence. The history of his escape is a recital of fearful interest.

After thirty-four years he now returns eastward to lay before Congress important facts connected with the early history of Oregon, and the fate of these communities by Indian barbarity and Jesuit intrigue.

Rarely, in the annals of human progress, does it fall to the lot of any man, as it has to this venerable pioneer, to go forth on foot and horseback and raft, by help of compass and axe, making his way across an unexplored continent, and having laid the foundations of States in the untrodden wilderness, to return a third of a century afterward over the whole distance by the luxury of the railway car, the old perilous journey of six months accomplished in six days.

Though worn and enfeebled in his long service and terrific sufferings, the narrative of this veteran and martyr missionary is one of intense interest to all who listen to it, well calculated to inspire the deepest respect for those apostolic men and women of all ages, our own not excepted, who have led the hosts of faith in the conquest **of** the world.

It adds to the interest that would naturally be felt in the presence of such a man in our community that the original company of missionaries was made up in Southern New York. Rev. Mr. Spalding and Mrs. Whitman were from Plattsburg, Dr. Whitman from Wheeler, and Mrs. Spalding from Holland Patent. Mr. Spalding was ordained at Big Flatts.

Honorable Mr. Allison's definition of an executive document.

We find in our executive documents here official communications from the officers of the Government which can alone speak officially upon the subject. (See General Lane's speech in the House of Representatives, April 2, 1856.)

Executive documents, then, are regarded and treated by Congress as official testimony. Executive documents, then, No. 38, of Thirty-fifth Congress, and No. 1, volume 2, of Thirty-seventh Congress, will be held as official testimony against the Protestant Church in the United States.

VI.—WHO INSTIGATED THE INDIANS TO MURDER THE MISSIONARIES AND AMERICANS?

IMPORTANT TESTIMONY.

Question. And further, from your acquaintance with Doctor and Mrs. Whitman, and with Mr. and Mrs. Spalding and from your knowledge of the results of their labors among the Indians, and the results and influence, both of Protestantism and of Roman and British influence in Oregon, can you not answer decidedly in the negative the following questions, which are mostly framed from verbatim extracts from said document, to-wit:

Has the American Congress the least shadow in truth to represent, as they do in said document, on page three, that the taking of the Indians' land by the missionaries (Whitman and Spalding) was one of the alleged causes of the murder of Dr. Whitman and family?

Answer. I believe and know this to be false.

GEORGE ABERNATHY.

The most wicked falsehood ever uttered.

A. HINMAN.

Whitman and Spalding took no lands, only the stations they occupied and improved, as the Indians requested them, and upon which they located them on arriving in the country in answer to a call from the Indians, and as authorized by a written permit by the War Department at Washington, dated March 1, 1836.

J. S. GRIFFIN.

In answering this question it is proper for me to state that Dr. Whitman went to Washington in the winter of 1842–'43 to prevent, if possible, the loss of Oregon to the United States; and while gone I was in charge of his station among the Cayuse Indians, who informed me on many occasions that the priests and half-breeds were urgent that they should drive Mr. Spalding and Dr. Whitman out of the country, so that they (the priests) could occupy the country and the places of Whitman and Spalding. I asked them on many different occasions if they wanted Messrs. Spalding and Whitman to leave their country after they had been there so long and taught them so much, both in religion and in civilization, and cultivating the soil, &c. They answered, "Oh, no; it is the priests that are continually desiring us to drive them away."

And again, in 1846 the priests became very urgent and the Catholic Indians became so noisy about the matter that the tribe held a great council about the matter. Doctor Whitman made them a speech. He told them his locks were getting gray. He had spent his best days in trying to do them good, but if they wished him to leave he would be ready to leave in two weeks.

After three hours of conference they made their reply as follows:

"When you first came to our country we knew nothing about cultivating the land and making a living in that way. We had no cattle, hogs, plows, or hoes. Now we have all these that you have assisted us to procure and taught us to use. Before you came we were always hungry in the winter; now we have plenty to eat and to spare. Formerly we knew but little of God; now we worship him every day in our families. After receiving so much we do not wish you to leave us but to stay with us as long as you live, and occupy the place that you now occupy."

I say most emphatically that the Jesuit priests then in this country were the true instigators of the murder of Doctor Whitman and those with him, and the Roman Catholic Indians the principal actors.

WM. GEIGER, Jr.

That country would have been much settled before now but for the efforts made by the lamented Doctor Whitman on behalf of the Cayuses to prevent it. His lips are now sealed in death; massacred by the bloody hands of those for whom he so long and so earnestly labored. We see no reason now why the Cayuse country should not be open to the settlement of the white man.—*Judge Wait, editor of Oregon Spectator, July* 13, 1848.

The same Spectator contains the proclamation of the superintendent of Indian affairs, throwing open the Cayuse country for settlements, showing, in connection with the above, that the missionaries, so far from inviting settlers to the Cayuse and Nez Perces countries, they discouraged it, and the citizens respected their wish up till the period of the massacre.

"In consideration of the barbarous and insufferable conduct of the Cayuse Indians, as portrayed in the massacre of the American families at Waiilatpu   *   *   *   and with a view to inflict upon them a just and proper punishment, as well as to secure and protect our fellow-citizens emigrating from the States,   *   *   *   after consultation with his excellency, George Abernathy, governor of Oregon Territory, I, H. A. G. Lee, superintendent of Indian affairs, hereby declare the territory of said Cayuse Indians forfeited by them and justly subject to be occupied and held by American citizens resident in Oregon.   *   *   *

In testimony of which I subscribe my name.

H. A. G. LEE,
Superintendent of Indian Affairs, Territory of Oregon.

INDIAN DEPARTMENT, OREGON CITY,
July 6, 1848.

Out of that gloom came up a voice, deep, clear, loud, yet single, for it was the voice of all, as of one, " These brutal murders must and shall be avenged."

Dr. Whitman's mission among the Indians was a mission of love; he and his worthy associates have spent years in faithful and active endeavors to improve the mental and moral condition of those Indians, and in the midst of that mission he, his worthy lady, and twelve Americans have fallen victims to Indian ingratitude and insatiable love of blood. Surely those brutal murders must and should be avenged.—*Judge Wait, editor of the Oregon Spectator, February* 16, 1848.

The war in which this little settlement is engaged has not been produced by the indiscretions of its members, nor by any infringement of nor by aggressions upon the rights of the Indians, but by Indian inhuman butcheries of unoffending citizens, induced by a thirst for the blood of the servants of the Living God.—*Judge Wait, editor of the Oregon Spectator, February* 24, 1848.

The Cayuse tribe, after committing numerous outrages and robberies upon the late emigrants, have, without semblance of provocation or excuse, murdered eleven American citizens. Among them were Dr. Marcus Whitman and his amiable wife, members of the American Board of Foreign Missions.—*Memorial of the legislative assembly of Oregon Territory to the Senate and House of Representatives of the United States, January,* 1848.

Mr. Speaker, could you read in the records of heaven the deeds of this power, (Hudson's Bay Company,) in Oregon, your whole moral nature would be shocked by the baseness of the designs and the means for their accomplishment. If a settler located anywhere against the company's will he had to pay the forfeit.

(Hearing of these projected plans in the United States, these Jesuitical rascals took the earliest means possible to head off the enterprises and to wrest the whole country from us and our Government.) Dr. McLaughlin received orders, as the governor of this western branch of this company, to dispatch agents to Fort Hall and order them to stop the American emigration, and, if possible, to prevent them from crossing the Blue Mountains. And if that lamented man, Dr. Marcus Whitman, had not been murdered, as well as papers burned, we should have had the evidence which this company feared.

Mr. Speaker, there is a tale about the murder of this Dr. Whitman of no little interest to this Hudson's Bay Company. When Whitman, who piloted the emigration of 1843, arrived at Fort Hall, when they found these men would not be deterred by any other means, they threatened to bar them by the Hudson's Bay Company, who had possession of the country and who would not allow them to settle. Of the murder of Dr. Whitman and that great number of American emigrants, which murder I have no more doubt was instigated by the Hudson's Bay Company than I doubt my existence.—*Hon. S. R. Thurston's speech in the House of Representatives, December 26, 1850.*

We entertain a very high respect for the Rev. H. H. Spalding. He left home and friends and comfort, and passed, with the wife of his choice, into a distant wilderness, to rear a family and wear out his own life and that of his estimable wife in teaching the arts of civilization and the glad tidings of salvation to the benighted savages.

Mr. Spalding and his associates own no property in Oregon. What they have grown and reared has been so much saved to and for the society whose stewards they are. We have seen a disposition to undervalue the objects and efforts of missionaries. This is wrong, and a moment's reflection will satisfy all of the injustice of imputing selfish motives to the missionaries. The importance of the country, as described by them, brought the citizens of Oregon here. We can readily see what brought the Hudson's Bay Company here; but *what brought the missionaries*, who, with their lives in their hands, led the way with their wives into this country, when it was almost unknown and entirely unappreciated? It would appear that there is but one answer; it was the high and holy estimation which they placed upon the importance of souls and the command of their Great Master in Heaven.—*Judge Wait, editor of the Oregon Spectator, July 13, 1848.*

2. On pages 18 and 27, that the missionaries promised the Cayuse and Nez Perces "to pay them every year for their lands;" also, "to come every year a big ship loaded with goods to be divided among the Indians; not to be sold, but to be given to them;" also, "plows and hoes, not to sold but given to you."

Answer. I believe this to be false.

GEO. ABERNATHY.

Their instructions from the board were directly the opposite.

J. S. GRIFFIN.

(See letter of Presbyterian Committee to Blakely.)

3. On page 27, " that the want of fulfillment of these promises was one of the true causes remote and immediate of the whole evil."

Answers. I believe this false.

GEO. ABERNATHY.

Slanders of the worst description.

J. S. GRIFFIN.

4. On pages 19 and 26, that "Dr. and Mrs. Whitman were severe and hard to them, (Indians,) and ill-treated them;" that Spalding and wife were so "bad" the "Nez Perces blockaded the missionaries" in the house "for more than a month;" that the Catholics were "sent three times to induce the Indians to set the missionaries at liberty."

Answers. I believe this all false.

GEO. ABERNATHY.

All the above charges against Dr. Whitman are untrue, I am certain. Dr. and Mrs. Whitman were good people, and lost their lives laboring for those who murdered them; and that the name of Mrs. Spalding will be cherished while a single Nez Perces remains.

R. NEWELL.

5. On page 28, that "missionaries worked only for themselves;" "refused obstinately from year to year to pay the price they had promised for their lands," and "persisted to keep them;" "neglected the Indians;" did, taught, helped, nor made "nothing for them unless they should be paid a great price."

Answers. Also false.

G. A.

A Jesuit slander, repeated by Congress, to their shame and the shame of all Americans.

J. S. GRIFFIN.

Totally untrue.

R. NEWELL.

6. On pages 3, 21, 22, 25, 28, and 31, that the Protestant missionaries produced " evil effects upon the Indians;" "instead of Christianizing the Indians, showed a very bad

example to the races;" "did not benefit the Indians;" "made them worse;" "neither taught, nor helped, nor furnished them with anything; neither written nor printed books; neither schools nor board, nor clothing for boarding children; no room or care for the sick; no medicine for the nation, and provided no saw or flour mill for the benefit of the nation; no shops, no church, no spinning and weaving room; helped them to nothing, neither seeds, plows, hoes, nor cattle; neither sheep, orchards, ditches, nor farms; never visited the sick, nor gave an Indian a piece of meat when hungry; neither translated nor printed for them any part of the Bible."

Answer. I believe all false. How any set of men could make such assertions I cannot understand, as they are directly opposed to the facts in the case.

GEO. ABERNATHY.

All slanders of the worst description; and it was only as the Jesuits were running Congress that that body ever published such scandal.

J. S. GRIFFIN.

Totally untrue.

WM. GEIGER, Jr.

7. On page 28, that "the missionaries (Whitman and Spalding) took their (Indians') horses, cattle, and grain," and "traded them to the emigrants," "without dividing with the Indians, and were getting rich."

Answer. Do not believe a word of it.

G. A.

A Jesuit slander, repeated by Congress.

J. S. GRIFFIN.

8. On pages 30 and 31, that "the applications of the missionaries to get excessive riches," "with excessive seeking for temporal welfare."

Answer. I believe the efforts of the missionaries were to elevate and benefit the Indians, not to obtain riches.

GEO. ABERNATHY.

Spalding and Whitman had not a dollar salary, and were allowed by the board to draw but $500 a year for each family, with which to do everything in that "great and terrible wilderness," destitute of everything, 200 miles from nearest mill, and 400 from shop or store, and with that to feed, clothe, house themselves, to do all missionary work, to put up shops, mills, churches, school-houses, and printing office, open farms, and keep all going.

J. S. GRIFFIN.

I think the missionaries were not allowed any salary, and were required to practice the most strict economy, in order to support their large families. Dr. Whitman had eleven children, (white.) Mr. Spalding had some twenty boarding children, (Indian,) beside the large Indian school.

A. HINMAN.

The missionaries (Spalding and Whitman) owned no property.—*Oregon Spectator of July*, 1848.

All these results were accomplished at an expense to the American Board of Missions of $500 per annum for each mission family; the enterprise and indefatigable industry of the missionaries did the rest with native help.—*Sacramento Union, July* 10, 1869.

In this lonely situation they (Spalding and wife) have spent the best part of their days for no other compensation than a scanty subsistence.

JOEL PALMER.

9. On pages 26, 22, and 23, that Dr. and Mrs. Whitman and Spalding "sent to the States for poison to kill the Cayuse and Nez Perces;" received poison by the emigrants that year; distributed it to kill tigers, as he (Whitman) "said, laughing," that Whitman and wife and Spalding were overheard to say "Such an Indian has so many horses, and such an Indian has so many spotted horses; when the Indians are all dead, our boys will drive them up, and we will give them to our friends, who will be on from the States and want to settle on these good lands, and we will live easy."

Answer. Any one that knew Dr. Whitman would at once say this is all untrue. It is probably made to turn attention from the true cause of the massacre.

GEORGE ABERNATHY.

The entire statements are as false as hell itself. So far as my means of information have enabled me to judge, there never has been one single incident from which any one of the above nine statements could have originated other than from a depraved heart, and with an intent to falsify.

JOEL PALMER.

My reply to the calumnies under the above nine statements is, to my personal knowledge it was entirely the reverse.

I. N. GILBERT.

The entire nine statements are perfectly false as can be.

P. H. HATCH.

These statements under these nine heads are maliciously false, to my personal knowledge, and made, as I believe, for no other purpose than to shift the responsibility of the Whitman massacre from those guilty Catholics to those who were as innocent as the President of the United States.

A. HINMAN.

Nothing further from the truth than the entire nine statements, and so proved at the time, and Congress was wofully ignorant that they did not know it.

J. S. GRIFFIN.

Now, therefore, it is resolved by this presbytery, that in the opinion of this presbytery, from a vast array of most reliable testimony now before us on the subject, the unfavorable statements made in this congressional document concerning the Protestent missionaries in Oregon are in the highest degree false and slanderous.— *Willamette Presbytery of the Cumberland Presbyterian Church, May, 1869.*

Your committee find, from overwhelming evidence from the testimony of different United States officers, civil and military, and from other citizens of most reliable credibility, that this congressional document has involved in it so many prominent and absolute falsehoods as to cast most fallacious and infamous reflectio s upon the characters of the elevated and faithful missionaries of the American Board there laboring at that time.— *Extract from resolutions adopted by the Congregational Association of Oregon, June, 1869.*

The notoriety which these atrocities speedily obtained naturally aroused the instigators to attempt at concealment, where secrecy could avail and at self-defense where the facts could be neither suppressed nor distorted. They have sought to exculpate themselves by various expedients, and especially in the publication above referred to, in which the character of Dr. Whitman and his associates is traduced, their motives assailed, their actions misrepresented, and thus a deliberate attempt is made to stigmatize the fame of men and women which is far above reproach, and whose services as patriots and philanthropists entitle them to the lasting gratitude of the nation.— *Extract from resolutions adopted by the Oregon Presbytery of the Old School Presbyterian Church, June, 1869.*

From personal knowledge, some of us being residents of the country at the time, and from overwhelming testimony, we are convinced that Romanism and British influence were the main causes of the Whitman massacre and the wars that followed, and of the persecuting and banishing from the country the Protestant missionaries, and of destroying their property and imperiling their health and lives. Romanism has, we are persuaded, with a bitterness unparalleled except in the past history of its own bloody acts, attempted, in every way possible to them, the utter subversion of Protestantism in Oregon.— *From the resolutions adopted by the Oregon Presbytery of the United Presbyterian Church, 1868–'69.*

But we reject this congressional "chapter on Protestant missions" with unutterable mortification as Americans, and with the deepest detestation as Protestants, and for the following reasons: 1st. Because it breathes on every page the most malignant bitterness against the Protestant Church. 2d. Because it is a libel on Oregon's history, and a gross calumny on Oregon's pioneers.— *From the Resolutions of the Pleasant Bute Baptist Church, Linn County, Oregon, October, 1869.*

These are the monsters who, with their hands red with the blood of American Protestants, receive a copyright from our American Congress to prepare testimony against, and chapters on, Protestant missions. But, as Oregonians, we reject this "chapter," and we respectfully advise Congress to burn it—to call in every one of the 75,000 volumes and burn them. You owe it to yourselves; you owe it to the age; you owe it to Oregon. The most significant and ominous feature of this whole affair is, not that the Indians could be induced to butcher their teachers; not that the Jesuit priests could pay down the savages on the spot for butchering the heretics, by baptizing their blood-stained children while the murders were going on, and by handing out, with their own hands, our helpless captive young women and infants to be the sport of the tomahawk and brutalities worse than death; not that they could meditate the destruction, by the tomahawk, of the entire infant settlements, to gloat their hellish hate of Protestantism and Americans, and actually did ship up the Columbia River a great quantity of ammunition for the combined savage hosts waiting at the Des Chutes for it, as they themselves announced three days before it arrived at the Dalles, where it was intercepted at the last critical moment. This is all in keeping with Romanism; but that Congress should offer this infamous document to the world as *"an interesting and authentic chapter in the history of Protestant missions."* This action of the Exective and of Congress speaks a language louder than words can utter. It is a direct insult to the Protestant Church.—*From the Report adopted by the Christian Church in Linn County, Oregon, October, 1869.*

Also, by the annual meeting of said body, for Oregon, in Polk County, in 1870.

These proofs, in the Oregon publications of the day, drew out a lengthy publication in the Freemen's Journal, New York, 1848, headed *"Protestanism in Oregon,"* given with all the sophistry of the Jesuit mind, and which directly attempted to show that the missionaries were horse thieves and poisoners, laboring only to make money out of the Indians, giving them no instruction, and continually breaking plighted faith with them. That they brought destruction upon themselves, and were entirely unworthy of confidence. The publication of it deserves little notice, only as it was embodied word for word in the report of J. Ross Browne, and published as an executive document by order of the House of Representatives, Thirty-fifth Congress, and went forth to the word a gross slander on American missionaries, who lost their lives in the cause they had espoused, and whose memories should be honored so long as the story of the early settlement of Oregon is told. There is no possible excuse for Mr. Browne. He either maliciously took this course to slander the memory of martyred dead, or he was too heedless of great principles and of the mission intrusted to him to give it conscientious performance.—*Sacramento Union, July,* 1869.

And this false narrative was, by Congress, published to the world, with no reply to its enormous statements. It is one of the strongest, shrewdest measures of the Jesuits of which we have read in American history, to get Congress to publish this narrative of over fifty pages, filled with most erroneous charges against the Protestant missionaries, trying to throw off from themselves the well-founded public belief that they were the real causes of this horrible massacre, and place the blame upon Americans. Also, that Browne should, from choice or otherwise, become a tool of these Jesuits to get Congress to publish the false account, virtually sanctioning it as true, and placing it alone among its permanent documents for future reference, is a fact that calls for unmeasured condemnation.—*The Pacific, of San Francisco, July 22,* 1869.

But to call attention to a great wrong that has been done the memory of these early Christian pioneers by the Congress of the United States. This insidious libel upon those devoted Christian martyrs was ingeniously palmed upon the Department of the Treasury by J. Ross Browne. The priest, Brouilette, wrote in the most malicious spirit, such as is expected of Rome. As for J. Ross Browne, he richly deserves to be held up to the scorn and contempt of every honest man for suffering himself to be made the mouth-piece for trumpeting forth a gross and malicious calumny against the most self-sacrificing band of Christian pioneers that ever braved the dangers of a pagan wilderness.—*American Unionist, Salem, Oregon, June 26,* 1869.

It is affirmed in this congressional document, that "these pages will form an interesting and authentic chapter in the history of Protestant missions." And in this 'chapter,' the Hon. J. Ross Browne took advantage of his position as an officer of the Government to advance the interest of the Catholic Church, by covering with obloquy the memory of those who sacrificed their lives for the promotion of republican liberty and Christian civilization, and of utterly destroying the character of the only survivor of that heroic band, the first to cross the Rocky Mountains and the continent with their wives, and the first to plant the seeds of pure Christianity in Eastern Oregon. We refer to the Rev. H. H. Spalding.—*From the manifesto adopted by the Oregon Conference of the Methodist Episcopal Church,* 1869.

Oregon owes too much to Protestant missions to allow such monstrous falsehoods to go without remonstrance. It is not generosity, nor eulogy of the memories of those who may truly be called the founders of the State, which is desired; it is simple justice. Let honor be given to whom honor is due.—*Pacific Christian Advocate.*

From Rev. Gustavus Hines, missionary and presiding elder, Methodist Episcopal Church.

SALEM, OREGON, *March* 22, 1869.

This is to certify that I arrived in Oregon in the spring of 1840; that I have been identified with the country most of the time since that period; that I have been cognizant of, and conversant with, all the early missionary establishments, both under the direction of Spalding and Whitman, in the interior, and of the Lees, in the valley of the Willamette, and that, according to the best of my knowledge, the extracts from congressional documents, as taken by the Rev. R. H. Spalding, involving the character of Dr. Marcus Whitman and wife, Mr. Spalding and wife, as well as others, are wholly and totally false. And I furthermore state that the missionaries referred to, instead of deserving the foul censures of the great American Congress, have been the greatest benefactors of the nation upon the Pacific coast.

GUSTAVUS HINES.

Question. On the other hand, did not the Catholic priests and the Hudson's Bay men oppose the settling of the country by American settlements from the beginning, and the formation of the provisional government?

Answer. This is my belief; they opposed the formation of the provisional government.

GEO. ABERNATHY.

That is my opinion.

P. H. HATCH

In every move to promote the settlement and internal improvement of Oregon, Dr. McLaughlin and the Hudson's Bay Company to a man have been opposed, until they were absolutely compelled by force of circumstances to yield. The history of that company in Oregon is no less oppressive and unjust, as regards American citizens, than was that of their ancestors in 1776.—*Hon. S. R. Thurston, in Congress, December,* 1850, *from a petition to Congress by 56 early Oregonians—G. Hines, Shortess, Bears, and others.*

From Dr. Treat, Secretary of American Board of Commissioners for Foreign Missions, 1870.

MASSACRE OF DR. WHITMAN—A CHAPTER IN AMERICAN HISTORY—HOW OREGON WAS SAVED TO THE UNITED STATES—WHO EXCITED THE INDIANS TO MURDER THE MISSIONARIES?

Nearly ten years ago a document was published at Washington which seems to have attracted very little notice at first—it may have done its appointed work, nevertheless—but which has caused within the last few months no small stir beyond the Rocky Mountains. It is known as Executive Document No. 38, House of Representatives, Thirty-fifth Congress, first session, and was printed by order of the House of Representatives. This document contains a "letter of J. Ross Browne, special agent of the Treasury Department, to the Commissioner of Indian Affairs, reviewing the origin of the Indian war of 1855–'56 in the Territories of Oregon and Washington."

This "letter" apparently, and nothing else, was called for by the House of Representatives; but we find, to our utter astonishment, after perusing its less than twelve pages, with grave questionings here and there, that we have come to an essay of more than fifty pages on "Protestantism in Oregon." We find, too, that this essay was written and published in the New York Freeman's Journal, by Rev. J. B. A. Brouilette, vicar general of Walla-Walla, some ten years before the date of Browne's letter. An American may be pardoned for asking, just here, why an ex-parte statement of such suspicious length, already before the world, should be appended to a "letter," addressed by a special agent of the Treasury Department to the Commissioner of Indian Affairs, and why especially it was *called* for and printed by the House of Representatives?

It is easy enough to understand the motives of Father Brouilette in writing this monograph, but it is not so easy to understand why it should have received such distinguished honor from Hon. J. Ross Browne and the House of Representatives. It was quite natural that Father Brouilette should wish to free himself and associates from blame; but why should the House of Representatives, so many years after, call for and give currency to his defense at public charges under the name of "Protestantism in Oregon?" The Congregational Association of Oregon adopted a report in June last which condemns the "prominent and absolute falsehood" of this document, and expresses the belief, "from evidence clear and sufficient to them," that the Roman Catholic priests did themselves instigate violence to the missions, resulting in the massacre. Similar action was taken by the Old School, the Cumberland, and United Presbyterian Presbyteries. The Methodist Conference, composed of more than seventy preachers, under the presidency of Bishop Kingsley, adopted a comprehensive and able report, in which the massacre at Waiilatpu is declared to have been "wholly unprovoked by Dr. Whitman or any member of the mission," and to have arisen from the policy of the Hudson's Bay Company "to exclude American settlers," and "the efforts of Roman priests directed against the establishment of Protestantism in the country." Other religious bodies have acted, it is believed, and valuable testimony is borne to the character of the missionaries. While the motives of Hon. J. Ross Browne in appending Father Brouilette's pamphlet to his "letter," and the reasons of the House of Representatives for publishing the same, are open to grave suspicions, facts have been elicited which throw light on the bearings and uses of the missionary enterprise.—*New York Evangelist, January 6, 1870.*

Important testimony of civil and military officers and old citizens and religious bodies.

WHO EXCITED THE INDIANS TO KILL DOCTOR WHITMAN AND WIFE AND OTHERS, AND TO DESTROY THE AMERICAN SETTLEMENT?

Question. Do not nineteen out of twenty of the Americans who were in the country at the time, believe that it was Romanism and British influence which caused the bloody massacre of Doctor Whitman and wife and the American emigrants who were butchered with them?

Answer. They could not believe otherwise. Had Romanism never come here the massacre never would have occurred.

GEO. ABERNATHY.

That is my opinion.

JOEL PALMER.

I know it to be so.

J. N. GILBERT.

I have no other opinion.

P. H. HATCH.

I so believe.

A. HINMAN.

The above sentiment was universal.

WILLIAM GEIGER, JR.

At that time I was editor of the Oregon American, and I am positive in my testimony that an overwhelming majority of the Americans held it as proved, that the Jesuit missionaries were the procuring cause of the Whitman massacre and the other Amercans who fell with him, and of the Indian wars that followed. So fully were the Jesuits convicted that no one has ever attempted a reply in Oregon in their behalf.

J. S. GRIFFIN.

That the causes of the massacre were reducible to two, viz, the purpose of the English government or of the Hudson Bay Company to exclude American settlers from the country, and the efforts of Catholic priests to prevent the introduction of education and of Protestantism by preventing the settlement of American settlements, and that the efforts which both parties made, operating on the ignorant and suspicious minds of the savages, led to the butchery in which twenty lives were destroyed, and the most dreadful sufferings and brutal injuries inflicted on the survivors.—*Oregon Presbytery, Old School Presbyterian Church, June 22, 1869.*

That the massacre was wholly unprovoked by Dr. Whitman, or any member or members of the mission.

That the true cause of the massacre may be found in the course and policy pursued by the Hudson Bay Company, which was an embodiment of the British Government at that time in the country, to exclude American settlers from the land, and the efforts of the Roman priests directed against the establishment of Protestanism in the country, which they hoped to accomplish by preventing its settlement by American citizens. These two things, a knowledge of which was possessed by the savages, excited them, doubtless, to perpetrate the horrid butchery, and to inflict upon the survivors the most indescribable brutalities.—*The Methodist Conference of Oregon, August,* 1869.

That from what is regarded as evidence of the most reliable character this presbytery is fully convinced that the Roman clergy then occupying the country were the principal instigators of the Whitman tragedy.—*Orange Presbytery of Cumberland Presbyterian Church, May,* 1869.

Your committee believe, from evidence clear and sufficient to them, that these Roman priests did themselves instigate violence to the mission, resulting in the massacre, and that this document, so strangely published by Congress, with no rebutting statements accompanying it, was prepared by them to throw the blame of the massacre upon the American missionaries.—*Congregational Association of Oregon, June,* 1869.

From personal knowledge and overwhelming testimony now before us, we, as a presbytery, are convinced that Romanism and British influence were the main causes of the Whitman massacre, the wars that followed, and the prosecuting and banishing from the country the Protestant missionaries, destroying their property and imperiling their lives.—*Oregon Presbytery of United Presbyterian Church,* 1868 and 1869.

Resolution adopted by the Christian Church of Oregon, at their annual meeting in Polk County, June, 1870.

But we reject this "chapter" on Protestant missions, or record of the court—if trial it is to be regarded, and such it will be, by a majority of readers—because of the irregular and extraordinary mode of proceeding, and

1. The so-called court had no jurisdiction in the case. The American Congress is not an ecclesiastical body, not even a judicial; but the case is purely religious, being Protestantism in Oregon.

2. It had no jurisdiction as to territory. The four scores and ten crimes or counts, as found in the bill of the indictment against the criminal, are set orth as committed in the Territory of Oregon; but the court sits in the city of Washington, 3,000 miles away,

thus repeating in this republican commonwealth the grievance loudest complained of by the fathers of 1776.

3. Three of the four individuals brought before the court for trial were dead, and had been for years; fell martyrs to that very Government which is thus tearing open their graves in Oregon, and taking them 3,000 miles to Washington to blacken them in their public documents; and the only survivor was not notified of said intended trial, (another breach of the Constitution,) consequently had no opportunity to confront the testimony or to offer testimony, and where more than property or life was at stake, (another breach of the Constitution,) and the court, even the United States Congress refused to appoint a counsel, which is always done in every court of the civilized world, even for the vilest of criminals.

4. There was no jury. Thus in several particulars the fundamental principles of the sacred Constitution of the United States are violated in this royal farce.

5. The character of the testimony which the court felt themselves authorized to accept in this trial of "Protestantism in Oregon," and the manner of collecting it caps the climax. Nothing like it in the history of any court of the civilized world, and fit rather for the dark ages of the Spanish inquisition, when black suspicion and hellish hate took the place of calm reason and truth.

Fifteen of the so-called witnesses were known to have been concerned in the horrible butchery, and must have been so known to the court, and which would have thrown their testimony out of any other court in the civilized world. Five of them had been tried and executed for the murder of Dr. Whitman. Nine statements put down in the testimony as the statements of General Joel Palmer and the Hon. Robert Newell, are proved by the testimony of these gentlemen, given to our committee, to have been forged against them. They never made such statements. And the whole of the so-called testimony is but Indian rumors passing through many hands.

*   *   *   *   *   *   *   *   *

We reject this so-called "chapter on Protestant missions," prepared at so great expense and sent forth to the world on the wheels of the Post Office Department as "an authentic chapter on Protestant missions,"(doubtless through some kind of smuggling,) to sadden the hearts of the children of the faithful dead and the friends of missions, because that from personal knowledge, some of us being in the country at the time, and from a vast array of testimony of the most unimpeachable character now before us, from old Oregonians, from eye-witnesses, from the captives, from military and civil officers, we are convinced that it was the Romish clergy and British agents working together to set on the Indians to destroy the American settlement and hand the country back to England, which instigated the massacre in which Dr. Whitman, his amiable wife, Mrs. Spalding, and seventeen others, mostly American emigrants stopping to winter and recruit, lost their lives, and the most brutal atrocities practiced upon female captives, reserved for a fate worse than death; the Protestant missions broken up, the last American forced to leave Middle Oregon, and the country involved in the long and most disastrous Indian wars.

6. Because this exective document, or so-called chapter on "Protestantism in Oregon," was written by one of the principal instigators of that most horrible butchery—a Jesuit by the name of I. B. A. Brouilette, the vicar-general of the papal hosts on this coast—and published in the Freeman's Journal, New York, a paper that has always proclaimed its hatred of Protestantism and our free schools and free press. This vicar-general was on the ground at Waiilatpu during the horrible butchery, which lasted eight days, with his bishop and thirteen priests, direct from Europe, camped at helping distance around, and with one of his overland party—an educated half-breed from Canada, by the name of Jo Lewis—at the window outside, by Dr. Whitman's head, to give the signal for the tomahawks to commence, who shot Mrs. Whitman through the breast, and with his own hands butchered Hoffman and two other Americans; who told the Cayuse and Oregon Indians he had seen, before he left the States, the letters of Spalding and Mrs. Whitman calling for poison to come by the emigrants to kill the Cayuse and Nez Perces. It was a question of life or death with them; they must destroy the Americans while few, or be destroyed. He would help them. The vicar-general and bishop, just over from the great father, the Pope, would furnish plenty of ammunition from the English posts. This Brouilette, to remove all doubt from the minds of the Oregon Indians as to his abhorrence of Americans, and as pay down to the savages for butchering the heretics, actually proceeded to baptize the blood-stained children of the murdering savages while the butchery was going on and the unburied dead and gasping bodies lay about his feet; hogs and dogs running about with parts in their mouths; the screams of our ever to be pitied young women, writhing in the hands of unrestrained brutality, his church music; and who, with his bishop and associates, handed over with their own hands our young helpless girls to be brutalized before their eyes, and turned our escaped fathers and infants and mothers out of their doors to be scalped by the savages, (see the testimony of Mr. Osborn, Miss Bewly, of George Abernathy, General Palmer, &c.;) and who, when our dear, helpless children and mothers were huddled in a corner, with blood-streaming tomahawks

brandished over their heads by the Indian women, crying to the chief, "Shall we strike?" rushed in among them, took a phial from the doctor's shelf, and holding it up to the excited Indians cried out through his Canadian helper, "Here is the identical poison; see what your Protestant Whitman and Spalding were doing; bury this or you are all dead." And our captives saw the box filled with earth, the phial put in as this priest directed, and taken off to be buried. (See testimony of C. Segor and Eliza Spalding, captives.) And all this to excite the savages to chop our helpless children and mothers to pieces on the spot. But the chief refused. And who, after all this; after the last Protestant missionary and American in Eastern Oregon had been killed or forced from the country, but his hate of Protestanism and of Americans, not yet sufficiently satisfied, could meditate the horrible butchery and attendant atrocities by the savages of the entire American settlements, and for that purpose actually shipped up the river from the English post at Vancouver over 3,000 pounds of powder and ball and boxes of guns, for the combined savages, and which was taken from them by Lieutenant Rogers and his little band of faithful Americans, only fifteen miles short of the camp of savages at Des Chutes, who had boasted only three days before that plenty of ammunition was coming by the priests for them, and then they would fall upon the American settlement and cut them off and take their women and cattle.

And while it remained a Romish production by such hands, no one took any notice of it, as the authors were totally unworthy of credit; but to our utter astonishment it now appears, word for word, in this "Ex. Doc.," and is offered to us by the American Congress, with an audacity that has no parallel in modern history, as "an interesting and authentic chapter in the history of Protestant missions." (Page 13, said document.) But we reject it with becoming American disdain, and as Protestants of this Pacific West we respectfully advise Congress to burn it—to call in, without delay, every one of those documents and burn them. You owe it to yourselves, to your country, and to the age.

JOHN M. HARRIS, Moderator.
W. H. ROWLAND. Clerk.

Question. Was not Romanism detected at Fort Wascopum (Dalles) in the attempt to transport a large amount of ammunition and arms up the Columbia, to furnish the upper savages, who were assembled at Des Chutes in great numbers, waiting, as they declared openly and defiantly, to receive it from the priests, and then fall upon the little garrison, and then come down upon the infant settlements and cut them off, and take their women and cattle as booty, and return and cut off the on-coming emigration of that fall?

Answers. It is true as to arms and powder being taken up by the priests, and seized at the Dalles. I ordered the muskets and ammunition sent back, and detained them at Oregon City until Governor Lane arrived.

GEO. ABERNATHY.

There were many events leading us to come to such conclusion.

J. PALMER.

Question. Was not over four thousand pounds of powder and balls, and three boxes of guns seized and taken from the priests at Fort Wascopum, fifteen miles short of this great camp of combined savages, by Lieutenant Rogers and his little band of fifteen, in 1848?

Answers. The powder and guns were seized by Lieutenant Rogers. He wrote me about it. I ordered them sent to me.

GEO. ABERNATHY.

There was a large amount taken from them, but I do not recollect the amount, or number of guns.

JOEL PALMER.

Question. Did not "Romanism in Oregon" pay down the savages for butchering the American heretics and for breaking up the American settlements, by baptizing the children of the savage murderers while they were actually killing, and the dead bodies of the slain lay about unburied, the food of hogs and wolves, and the screams of our captive young women in the hands of unrestrained brutality his church music; and by giving, with their own hands, our captive girls into the hands of the savages to be their wives; and by turning escaped Americans and their little children out of their posts, to be scalped by the Indians?

Answers. This is what I heard at the time.

GEO. ABERNATHY.

The Indians admitted and the captives asserted that the children of the murderers were baptized as stated, and the captive girls were given by the priests to some of the chiefs; and persons were refused admittance into the Hudson's Bay Company's post by McBean; and Hall was killed after being turned out.

JOEL PALMER.

Question. Have we not had to fight all the tribes on this northwest coast, as Colonel Nesmith reported when superintendent of Indian affairs, who have been under Romanism?

Answers. This has been the case.

GEO. ABERNATHY.

Nearly all, I believe.

JOEL PALMER.

I was in command of the Oregon volunteers in 1855–'56 when there was a concert of action with all the tribes on the northwest coast against the Americans, except the Nez Perces alone, who have always been friendly. In 1856, they furnished several hundred horses to remount my command.

T. CORNELIUS.

Question. Were not yourself and counsel fully convinced that the strongest efforts were made to induce the Nez Perces to join the combined hosts?

Answers. That is my opinion.

G. A.

Question. What would have been the consequences had they joined?

Answer. Had all the tribes joined, the Americans would have been destroyed.

GEO. ABERNATHY.

A chief of the upper Nez Perces has killed thirty head of cattle at a feast given to the nation, and this not being sufficient, seven more were killed. This was to unite all the hearts of the Indians together, to make war with the Americans. The cause of this war is that the Americans are going to seize their lands.—*Letter of Priest Paudozi Yankmiman, April,* 1853. *J. Ross Browne's Report,* 64.

Question. Did not Romanism defy our infant Government, and keep her missionaries in that middle country among the tribes who declared war upon the Americans, and after it was closed by Government against all missionaries alike?

Answer. I think the history of that day proves this.

GEO. ABERNATHY.

Yes, that is true.

JOEL PALMER.

And these are the hands, red with the blood of American mothers and daughters, whose productions, published ten years before and filled with forgeries upon Oregon's best citizens and with self-evident falsehoods to exculpate their own heads and to cast the blame on the memory of their victims, are called for by vote of Congress and ordered printed; (doubtless by some unfair means, but nevertheless its power as a state paper for evil remains the same.)

It is easy enough to see why Father Brouilette should wish to free himself and his associates from the well-founded belief that they were working with the Hudson's Bay Company to bring about the Whitman massacre, to break up the American settlements, and to hand the country back to England. But why should the American Congress, ten years after, call for Father Brouilette's ex-parte statements, and, at public charge, publish them under their seal and sanction and under the significant heading "Protestantism in Oregon?" And above all, why should such a burlesque on the cherished religion of the mass of the people of the United States be designated thus—(see page 13 said document:) "These pages will form an interesting and authentic chapter in the history of Protestant missions."—*Resolutions of Pleasant Bute Baptist Church.*

J. W. WARMOUTH.

J. C. H. Averill,
L. C. Rice,
H. R. Powel,
 Committee.

I do not take the religious view of this subject, but the policy view. It is a notorious fact that Mr. Spalding is the last Protestant Indian missionary, and his old home at Lapwai the last Protestant Indian mission in a large territory of the United States, while several Jesuit mission claims and more than a dozen Jesuit missionaries remain unmolested in the same country. Is it not clearly the duty of the American Government to protect the equal rights of all its citizens?—*From a letter of Hon. Anderson Cox to his excellency Governor Ballard, of Idaho.*

Convinced that the said executive document has had much to do in causing the expulsion of our brother Spalding from his native church; therefore,

Resolved finally, That the seizing by the Government of the old Protestant mission among the ever loyal Nez Perces, in 1862, driving off the American Board, in the person of their attorney, by force, pulling down the old missionary's house in 1863, forcing the board a second time from their lands, and in 1866 forcing the old missionary, the remnant of that heroic band of 1836, who had rendered such service to their country and to the early emigrants, and who himself had given his services and the best of his life to create enlightened loyalty in the breasts of the Nez Perces nation—our own brother beloved—from his old home, his orchards, mills, and farm—his home by the solemn acts of Government, by actual possession for thirty years, and until forced away, made sacred by the oft displays of God's converting grace. and by being the birth-place of all his children, thus consecrating it to Christ and to freedom by joys and by tears, by prayers, and by blood; and from his beloved people for whom himself and angel wife had abandoned all and left the joys and protection of civilized life long years before Government made foot-prints upon these shores; and from his beloved church of nearly thirty years' pastorate, and steadily keeping him away by force; and this, too, in the face of a strong memorial, repeated for three years, signed by over a thousand of the best citizens of Oregon and Washington respectfully asking Government to be allowed to renew the work of Christian missions among the loyal Nez Perces at Lapwai, but which petition has been steadily denied, thus virtually driving and keeping the Presbyterian Church out of five Territories of the United States, confiscating the lands of an old religious corporation of over fifty years, driving a Protestant pastor from his church, converting the house of God into a horse-stable, the school-room into a public brothel, steadily depriving a Christian people of the Sabbath administrations and the word of God; undoubtedly the first record of such defiant and long-continued outrages upon the Protestant church in the history of our Government, are well calculated to create the most serious apprehensions in the breast of every right-feeling man.   And the more especially as the Lapwai mission is the last Protestant Indian mission, and our brother Spalding the last Protestant Indian missionary in five Territories, while some fifteen Jesuit mission stations, most of them taken in defiance of the order of Government, and some twenty-three Jesuit missionaries, remained unmolested in the same field, and some of them known to be the identical instigators of the horrid massacre of American missionaries and American citizens above described, who paid the savages down for butchering the heretics by baptizing the children of the murdering savages while the slaughter was going on, and by handing over our helpless girls to be made the victims of savage lust, and our infants and mothers to be scalped, and who were detected at the Dalles, by Lieutenant Rogers, in attempting to furnish the combined savages with large quantities of ammunition with which to butcher and destroy the last American family in Oregon.

Done by order of the Christian Church, at Brownsville, Oregon, October 29, 1869.

JOHN M. HARRIS,
Moderator.
WM. H. ROWLAND,
Clerk.

Obadiah Tharp,
D. H. Putman,
Joseph Huntsaker,
Wm. H. Rowland,
      Committee.

THIRTY-SEVENTH AND THIRTY-NINTH CONGRESSES vs. OREGON'S HISTORIC DEAD.

Permit of the War Department.

WAR DEPARTMENT, OFFICE OF INDIAN AFFAIRS,
March 2, 1836.

SIR: At the request of the Rev. Mr. Greene, of Boston, Massachusetts, I enclose to you a permit for yourself and Doctor Marcus Whitman to reside in the Indian country among the Flathead and Nez Perces Indians.

Very respectfully, your humble servant,

ALBERT HERRING.

Rev. H. H. Spalding,
    St. Louis, Missouri.

The American Board of Foreign Missions have apprised the Department that they have appointed Doctor Marcus Whitman and Rev. Henry H. Spalding, both of the State of New York, to be missionaries and teachers to reside in the Indian country among the Flathead and Nez Perces Indians.

Approving the designs of said board, these gentlemen are permitted to reside in the country indicated, and I recommend them to the officers of the Army of the United States, to the Indian agents, and to the citizens generally, and request for them such attentions and aid as will facilitate the accomplishment of their object and protection, should circumstances require it.

Given under my hand and the seal of the War Department this 1st day of March, 1836.

LEWIS CASS.

Act of Congress confirming the land to the board, approved August 14, 1848.

"That the title to the land, not exceeding 640 acres, now occupied as mission stations among the Indian tribes in said Territory, together with the improvements thereon, be confirmed and established in the several religious societies to which said missionary stations respectively belong." (See Oregon Stats., 1855, page 39.)

Repeated by Government, determined to do justice to the mission boards, March 2, 1853.

"That the title to the land, not exceeding 640 acres now occupied as mission stations among the Indian tribes in said Territory, or that may have been so occupied as missionary stations prior to the passage of the act establishing the territorial government of Oregon, together with the improvements thereon, be and is hereby confirmed in the several religious societies to which said mission stations respectively belong." (Approved March 2, 1853.)

The act speaks for itself.

"Permit me to remark that a grant of public land by statute is the highest and strongest form of title known to our land. It is stronger than a patent."—*Opinion of Attorney General Bates, May* 29, 1864.

But neither statutory grants, opinion of Attorney General, nor possession of thirty years, nor blood of martyred patriots, are regarded now.

H. H. SPALDING.

THIRTY-SEVENTH, THIRTY-NINTH, AND FORTY-FIRST CONGRESSES vs. PROTESTANTISM IN OREGON.

WITNESSES FOR THE DEFENSE.

His excellency George Abernathy, governor of Oregon Territory at that date; Hon. Joel Palmer, commissioner general and superintendent Indian affairs at that date, and late United States superintendent of Indian affairs for Nez Perces Nation, and member of Oregon senate; Hon. R. Newell, Hon. A. Hinman; Messrs. J. N. Gilbert, P. H. Hatch; Revs. J. S. Griffin, H. H. Spalding, Horace Heart; Mrs. Mary Clymer; William Geiger; the Oregon conference of the Methodist Episcopal Church, 1869; the Oregon presbytery of the Old School Presbyterian Church, 1869; the Oregon presbytery of the United Presbyterian Church, 1868; Oregon Association of the Congregational Church, 1869; the Oregon Association of the Christian Church, 1869.

Whereas the House of Representatives, 3d session of the Thirty-seventh Congress, in executive document No. 1, vol. II, page 570, publishes as follows:

"As it is currently understood, by those in the country at the time, that the missionaries [Mrs. H. H. Spalding] voluntarily abandoned the claim [Lapway mission] on the 4th of December, 1847, and went into other business;"

And whereas the Government upon the above allegation proceeded to violate a solemn contract of a former administration for the use of said mission for twenty years as an agency, and proceeded to jump said mission claim and to drive the said American board off in the person of their attorney, Rev. C. A. Eells, in 1862, and to force the old missionary in 1865 from his old home, mills, orchards, from the beloved people and large schools, and from his native church of thirty years' pastorate and tore down his house; and whereas the Government has continued to keep forcible possession of said mission and property from that date to this, thus inflicting damage upon said American board which cannot be estimated, and upon that Nez Perces church and people who have rendered such invaluable service to the American people and American Government—a wrong which can never be redressed—by depriving them thus, year after year, of the Sabbath services and ministrations of their old pastor. And upon that pastor and most faithful missionary—the oldest clergyman upon the Pacific coast—a malicious outrage, a living death, an injustice that can never be amended, by driving him thus from his home; a home secured to him by three solemn acts of that Government; a home sacred to him by the oft displays of God's converting grace, and where himself and sainted wife gave the best of their life services to create in the breasts of the Nez Perces nation steadfast loyalty to the American people and Government; a home where were born all his children, and by driving him from his beloved church of thirty years' pastorate—gathered into the fold of Christ in that lone land long years ago—and by thus placing the brand of infamy upon his Christian character; and especially thus inflicting in this specified date a most sacrilegious, baseless, vandalic libel upon the memory of one who on the page of Oregon's history stands among the very few of the most eminently successful and devoted of modern missionaries, and whose heroic transit, in company with her equally heroic companion, Mrs. Marcus Whitman, of the North American continent, in 1836, over the Rocky Mountains, through the burning sand deserts, expecting to be two years, and to winter in the eternal snows and deep defiles of the mountains; to do without bread; to ask their daily food of God and receive it at the hands of the huntsman from the bands of the wild buffalo; the endurance of the horse to hold out the whole journey, and escape foes and starvation, their dependence—liable every moment to be pounced upon by the sleepless savage, scalped, taken prisoner, or put on foot to starve; sick or well, compelled to travel on without house or shelter, new dangers and toils multiplying upon every step, where so many strong men had perished, and where foot of white women had never trod—an undertaking pronounced impossible by mountain men and travelers for a white woman—will be by the impartial historian counted among if not the principal step that secured this great Pacific coast to the American people, as it demonstrated the all-important question that families and wagons could cross; thus by their personal hazards and foot-steps they established the overland emigrant route, and thus settled the Pacific slope with American settlements; this led to the development, and by American hands, of the endless gold fields so long hid from the eye of mortals, and to the great transcontinental railroad, and whose memory will be cherished both by the red and the white man while a single one remains alive of the Nez Perces race, or the story of the settlement of Oregon is told:

Resolved, therefore, That the truth of history, as also the immediate interest of the Protestant Church on these shores, and the honor of men and women whose characters are above reproach, demands a vindication at the hands of those who are familar with full facts; to this end, therefore, we, the committee appointed to examine the executive documents above referred to, would beg leave to propound to your excellency the following questions:

Question. The Government has published in the congressional documents and spread wide through the land to the damage of the defendant that it was currently understood by those in the country at the time that the said defendant voluntarily abandoned the said Lapway mission on the 4th of December, 1847. Was it so understood in this country at that time or at any time?

Answers.—

The missionaries were ordered to leave the country and forbidden to return to their missions.

GEO. ABERNATHY.

It was not so understood; it was deemed improper for Mr. Spalding and family to remain in that country until quiet was restored. It was not a voluntary abandonment of the station. We sent troops to escort Eells and Walker out of the country.

JOEL PALMER.

The best information that we have had by those present says it is false.

WM. GEIGER.

I was with the escort, and Mr. Palmer's statement is true.

J. M. GILBERT.

An escort was sent to bring those missionaries out of the Indian country.

P. H. HATCH.

I made no such representations.

R. NEWELL.

In no sense true.

J. S. GRIFFIN.

The above delaration in the above-said congressional docment is not true in any sense. The mission claim was not so abandoned on said 4th of December, 1847, or at any time, and it was not so understood by those in the county at the time.

H. H. SPALDING.

Deposition before the court of the third judicial district of Oregon, July 5, 1868, as called for by the court of the first judicial district, Idaho Territory, to give testimony in the case wherein the American Board of Commissioners for Foreign Missions is plaintiff, and the United States Government defendant.

HORACE HEART, of the county of Walla-Walla, Washington Territory, first being duly sworn, says: I was stopping with my brother-in-law, Rev. H. H. Spalding, in the fall of 1847. Mr. and Mrs. Spalding were missionaries of the American Board of Commissioners for Foreign Missions, and had been residing at Lapway, among the Nez Perces, since 1836, the year they crossed the mountains. Sometime in November Mr. Spalding and daughter, ten years of age, left home for Dr. Whitman's mission. On the 2d of December Mr. Canfield arrived at Lapway wounded in the side, and reported the sad news that Dr. and Mrs. Whitman, and all the American emigrants at Waiilatpu (Whitman's station,) were killed by the Indians; that Mr. Spalding was probably among the slain. That the women and children, his own wife and children, and Mr.

Spalding's daughter were made prisoners and reserved for a fate worse than death. That the the savages in council had determined to exterminate all Americans on the Pacific coast. That a large party of forty of the murderers were holding a scalp-dance only twelve miles distant, and would immediately be upon the station to commit a second slaughter. My sister threw herself at once upon her people, (the Nez Perces,) who immediately collected their forces to protect their much-beloved teacher, but decided they could not do it so well at the old station, where wood and grass were gone, as at a point of timber ten miles distant, where were both and timber to fort. This was late Saturday night. Mrs. S. refused to move on the Sabbath. This, though regarded by the four white men too superstitious, seemed wonderfully to inspire her Nez Perces. The chief said: "Now we know your religion is true; if you keep the Sabbath we will keep you;" and for some unaccountable reason the murdering party did not show themselves till Monday morning, the 4th of December. As we were leaving the station to seek the point of timber, they attacked us. But by this time a large force of Nez Perces had collected, and by their steady courage and the interposing hand of Providence we were saved, women and children.

On the ninth day after the slaughter at Waiilatpu had commenced, Mr. Spalding, to the utter atonishment but great joy of us all, was brought in by the Nez Perces, more dead than alive, from starvation, want of sleep, freezing, horrible swelled and mangled feet, having miraculously escaped the tomahawk at the first meeting of the murderers and priest, and traveled the whole distance of 180 miles by night of Egyptian darkness, hid days; half the distance on foot, his horse escaping, and barefoot, feeling his way over frozen ground, ice, snow, cut rocks, and prickly pear; no food, no sleep for six days. There were now with us five white men, two white women, and three children. On the 26th of December we received an express from Mr. Ogden, of the Hudson Bay Company, urging Mr. Spalding and all Americans to lose no time in joining him at Fort Walla-Walla, as our only hope of escaping from the country. This had been our only hope, and we regarded it a striking providence. We left on the 28th of December under an escort of fifty Nez Perces and reached Fort Walla-Walla 1st of January, 1848. Mr. Ogden, by almost superhuman efforts, had succeeded in ransoming all the captives at Waiilatpu, some sixty who had been brought in the day before. The next day he embarked with all on board of three boats for Oregon City, and delivered us all safe to the governor on the 12th of January.

HORACE HEART.

Subscribed and sworn to before me at my office, this 18th day of August, 1865. In testimony whereof I have hereunto set my hand and the seal of the district court of the first judicial district of Washington Territory.

B. F. SEXTON,
Clerk District Court.

State of Oregon, *County of Marion, ss:*

I have read the statements of Mr. Heart. I was present on the occasion, and believe them to be true.

MARY CLYMER.

Subscribed and sworn to before me this 14th day of December, 1868, at my office at Salem, Oregon. Witness my hand and seal.

R. C. GEER,
Clerk County Marion, State of Oregon.

Dayton, Oregon, *March* 2, 1852.

Having any regard for the safety of yourself and family, nothing could have induced you to neglect the opportunity afforded by Mr. Ogden, by which you were all taken out of the country.

A refusal, on your part, to have left at that time would have been regarded as a mark of insanity. * * * * * There were two things lacking on your part to render your stay safe in the country, to wit, a British subject or a member of the Catholic Church.

JOEL PALMER.

Rev. H. H. Spalding.

It also appears very clear by the accumulated evidence in the case that the Protestant missionaries among the Nez Perces and other tribes of the interior were compelled from the same cause to abandon their different fields of labor, while the missionaries of the Roman Catholic Church remain in perfect safety among the savages, in the immediate vicinity of the scenes of blood and carnage already described.

BISHOP KINGSLEY,
Moderator Oregon Conference M. E. Church, 1868.

Question. Were not the missionaries—the few who escaped—forced to leave their stations and the country to save themselves and children?
Answers. That was so.

GEORGE ABERNATHY.

Yes.

JOEL PALMER.

Yes.

J. N. GILBERT.

Yes.

P. H. HATCH.

Question. Were not Mrs. Spalding and her infant children (husband and daughter supposed to be slain) taken from her house, on the 4th of December, by the Nez Perces, to a point of timber ten miles to the fort, and saved their lives?
Answers. That is a statement of all Indians and whites.

WILLIAM GEIGER.

True, according to abundant proof at that time.

J. S. GRIFFIN.

Question. Was not every American missionary, who escaped, purchased of the Indians and taken out of the country by P. S. Ogden, of the Hudson Bay Company, and the volunteers?
Answers. P. S. Ogden, of the Hudson Bay Company, went up and rescued all that were left, and brought them down.

GEORGE ABERNATHY.

Yes, they were.

W. GEIGER.

Yes.

Mr. OGELEN,
Chief Fact. H. B. Co.

Purchased the captives.

JOEL PALMER.

True that Ogden redeemed them. They were held as hostages by the Indians to protect themselves against forces they feared might leave the valley and come against them.

J. S. GRIFFIN.

Question. And was not the country closed against all the missionaries alike by Government and the orders served on the Catholic mission and published in the Oregon Spectator of July 13, 1848; and was not the act of Congress, confirming the title of the mission lands to the respective mission boards, approved August 14 of the same year, and while the war continued and while the country remained closed?
Answer. The missionaries were ordered to leave and were forbidden to return, and the order was published, but I do not remember the date.

GEORGE ABERNATHY.

I do not remember dates, but it was understood that all missionaries and other Americans were prohibited residence in that country.

JOEL PALMER.

It was closed against Protestant missionaries, and the act of Congress took place while the war lasted and while the country was closed.

J. N. GILBERT.

Yes.

P. H. HATCH.

The country remained closed and the war continued till long after the act of Congress confirming the title of Lapway mission to the American Board.

W. GEIGER.

Mr. Geiger's statements are correct.

J. S. GRIFFIN.

The blood of the Whitman martyrs should have sanctified the equity of the claim.—*Governor Evans of Olympia.*

And would in the heart of every American who values Oregon or his own honor.

H. H. SPALDING.

It was not so understood. It was deemed improper for Mr. Spalding and family to remain in that country until quiet was restored. It was not a voluntary abandonment of the mission.　We sent troops to escort Rev. Messrs. Eells and Walker out of that country.

JOEL PALMER,
Commissioner General, Superintendent Indian Affairs.

WASHINGTON, *February* 1, 1871.

The bold, patriotic, and just action of President Grant in wresting the Nez Perces nation from the hands of those they have so long regarded their enemies, having, as they believed, deprived them of their teachers, and giving them back to their old friends, receives the approbation of every patriot in the land.　It is to be hoped the faithful, patriotic dead, who have been placed so long under brand of infamy, will be remembered next.

H. H. SPALDING.

VII.—RESOLUTIONS IN ANSWER TO EXECUTIVE DOCUMENT NO. 38 OF THE THIRTY-FIFTH CONGRESS,

Passed by five Protestant bodies of Oregon, to wit: D. The Oregon presbytery of the United Presbyterian church.　C. The Oregon presbytery of the Cumberland Presbyterian Church.　B. The Oregon presbytery of the Reunited Presbyterian Church.　E. The Congregational Association of Oregon.　F. The Oregon annual conference of the Methodist Episcopal Church.　G. The Pleasant Bute Baptist Church of Oregon.　H. The Christian Brotherhood of the State of Oregon.　I. Resolutions of the Steuben presbytery of Presbyterian Church, New York.　J. Memorial of the citizens of Steuben, Alleghany, and Chemung Counties, New York.　K. Memorial of the citizens of Oberlin, Ohio.

DOC. B.—The Whitman massacre.

RESOLUTIONS ADOPTED BY THE OREGON PRESBYTERY OF THE OLD SCHOOL PRESBYTERIAN CHURCH.

The presbytery of Oregon, at its session at Albany, on the 26th of June, 1869, took into consideration certain statements contained in Ex. Doc. No. 38 of the Thirty-fifth Congress, containing a report of the Hon. J. Ross Brown on the Indian war in Oregon and Washington Territories, into which is incorporated a paper prepared by the Rev. J. B. A. Brouilette, a Roman Catholic missionary, purporting to give a history of the massacre of Marcus Whitman, M. D., and others, at Walla-Walla, in the year 1847.

The object of the paper appears to be to exculpate the instigators of that tragedy, and to cast the blame on the victims.

The truth of history, as well as the character and services of Dr. Whitman and his coadjutors, demands a vindication at the hands of those who are familiar with the facts; especially since the above-named paper has been published by the authority of Congress.

Prior to the establishment of our national sovereignty over Oregon, (a term then applied to all our Pacific domain north of California,) and while the Hudson Bay Company, steadily working in the interest of Great Britian, were allowed to carry on their operations throughout that vast region, our Government desired to introduce settlers and cultivate amicable relations with the natives.　At the same time the Christian citizens sought to introduce the gospel, with the arts of civilized life, and thus, without any express understanding on the subject, the missionaries came to be the best agents of the Government.

Messrs. Whitman, Spalding, Walker, Eells, Gray, and others, clothed with the official protection of Government as citizens, and sent forth by the American Board of Commissioners for Foreign Missions, established themselves among the savages at different points in Middle Oregon in the years 1836 and 1838.　Besides ministers of the gospel there were teachers, farmers, mechanics, a printer, and physician, Dr. Whitman.　The ladies connected with these missions were well qualified to assist in promoting the sole object for which the entire company had left the enjoyments and protection of civilized life—the introduction of Christian civilization among the savages.

During the eleven years which followed, a great, and in many respects very gratifying improvement was made in the condition of the Indians.　The patient, laborious, and self-denying exertions of the missionaries were bearing precious fruit.　Agriculture and some of the mechanic arts had been acquired by the Indians; education and religion were exerting their benign influences, softening the savage disposition and elevating their character.　The mission had become an oasis in the desert—the resort of the emigrants to rest and recruit.　All the elements of modern civilization were transplanted and many steps of progress taken, notwithstanding the steady opposition and hostility which the agents of all these improvements had to encounter, and which culminated in the horrid butchery at Waiilatpu. The facts pertaining to this tragedy, attested by survivors, and by military and civil officers who have investigated them, as well as by Indians, furnishing a vast array of unimpeachable testimony supported by general consent, all go to show—

I. That the massacre was wholly unprovoked by Dr. Whitman or any member of the mission: on the other hand, the atrocity was deepened by the fact that at the time of its occurrence the martyrs were devoting their energies to the relief of those who were suffering from an epidemic disease then prevailing among the Indians, of unusual fatality.

II. That the causes of the massacre were reducible to two, viz: the purpose of the English government or of the Hudson's Bay Company to exclude American settlers from the country, and the efforts of the Catholic priests to prevent the introduction of education and Protestantism by preventing the settlement of American citizens, and that the efforts which both parties made, operating on the ignorant and suspicious minds of the savages, led to the butchery in which twenty lives were destroyed and the most dreadful sufferings and brutal injuries inflicted on the survivors.

III. That as incidental proof of the two-fold purpose above specified, American emigrants on their way toward the coast, then stopping at the mission premises, fell victims to the barbarities alike which were inflicted on the mission company.

IV. That in consequence of the massacre, not only was Dr. Whitman's mission destroyed, but, contrary to the statements of the Thirty-seventh Congress, the American missionaries among the neighboring tribes of the Spokanes and Nez Perces were compelled to abandon their fields of labor, being exposed to the same dangers; while the Catholic misionaries remained in perfect safety in the neighborhood of the scene of the massacre, mingled freely with the perpetrators of these deeds of horror, performed rites for the living which could have been postponed until they had paid decent respect to the martyred dead which lay around them "prone and discomposed" as they fell, and made no effort to arrest the brutal treatment of female survivors reserved for a fate worse than death.

The notoriety which these atrocities speedily obtained naturally aroused the instigators to attempts at concealment where secrecy could avail, and at self-defense where the facts could be neither suppressed nor distorted. They have sought to exculpate themselves by various expedients, and especially in the publication above referred to, in which, in the midst of a mass of trivial matter, the character of Dr. Whitman and his associates is traduced, their motives assailed, their actions misrepresented; and thus a deliberate attempt is made to stigmatize the fame of men and women which is far above reproach, and whose services as patriots and philanthropists entitle them to the lasting gratitude of the nation.

Let it not be forgotten that our republic is indebted to the enlightened patriotism of Marcus Whitman, who heroically defied the dangers of a winter's journey across the continent, and by the communication of important facts to the Government prevented the cession of a large portion of our Pacific domain to Great Britain; neither let the country forget Whitman's compatriots, who gave their services and their lives to create enlightened loyalty in the red man's breast. Their influence, and especially the arduous and long-continued labors of Mr. and Mrs. Spalding, secured fidelity and devotion to our country among the Nez Perces, the most powerful tribe west of the Rocky Mountains. During the Indian wars which followed the Whitman massacre, the Nez Perces were always true, and by their influence over other tribes they often saved our frontiers from being drenched in the blood of our citizens, and marked with the atrocities of savage warfare.

Let not the country cast dishonor on unselfish patriotism. Let not the brand of infamy remain on the memory of the just.

The publication of the allegations above mentioned, by authority of Congress, doubtless through one of those inadvertencies which sometimes creep into the proceedings of deliberative bodies, calls for ample redress. We therefore unite with all patriotic and fair-dealing men in the earnest petition that the Congress of the United States should do justice to the memory of the dead, and protect the rights of the living.

Adopted by presbytery.

A. L. LINDSLEY, Moderator.

Attest: E. R. GEARY, Stated Clerk.

Sad and interesting relics.

Lying before us is a collection of relics of the earliest work of the Christian missionary to plant the standard of his faith on this coast. There is the book of Matthew, printed in the Nez Perces language, at the Clear Water mission, in 1845, by M. G. Foisy; a copy of a small hymn-book, printed in 1842, and a speller and reader, printed in 1839, and designed for "children and new beginners." In addition to these there is a lock of hair, of considerable size, from the head of Mrs. Whitman, who was murdered by the Indians in 1847, near Walla-Walla. The hair is of silken texture and of a bright auburn color, indicating the sanguine temperament, with, perhaps, a shade of the nervous.   These relics are the property of Rev. H. H. Spalding, and it is through his kindness that we have been permitted to examine them.

In looking upon these sad mementoes of the past, we are carried back in the history of the progress of civilization to this land of the Occident, to the time when those heroic spirits, Spalding, Whitman, and their wives, braved the dangers of the savage wilderness and unfurled the banner of the Cross three thousand miles from home and friends, and when no succor could reach them other than that invoked from the God they worshipped.

"In the dreary depths of the pathless wild
  Where the mournful breezes moan,
And the stealthy step of the forest child
  Scarce wakes an echo-tone;
There the Christian chief hath boldly borne
  Redemption's blessed sign,
And the savage weeps o'er the crown of thorn
  And the Cross of love divine."

But we did not commence this article for the purpose of becoming sentimental, but to call attention to a great wrong that has been done the memory of those early Christian pioneers by the Congress of the United States.   We refer to the incorporation of the pamphlet published in 1848, by J. B. A. Brouilette, a Catholic priest, in Executive Document No. 38, Thirty-fifth Congress, 1st session, House of Representatives.   This insidious libel upon those devoted Christian martyrs was ingeniously palmed upon the Department of the Treasury and the Commissioner of Indian affairs, by J. Ross Browne, who, in 1857, visited this coast as special agent for those Departments.   Brouilette wrote in the interest of the Roman cause, and could not be expected to give an unprejudiced account of the causes which induced the massacre at the Whitman station.   But Browne being himself a member of the order of Jesuits, took advantage of his position in the service of the Government to advance the interest of his Church at the expense of the memory of the dead.   We say this in no spirit of animosity toward the character of the Roman Church, but in vindication of the memory of those who sacrificed their lives in the advancement of the cause of republican liberty and Christian civilization.   There are soldiers in peace as well as in war; and though no waving plume beckons them on to glory and to death, their dying scene is oft a crimson one.   They fall leading the vanguard of civilization along untrodden wilds, and they are buried beneath the dust of its advancing columns.   No stone marks their last resting place, the winds alone sing their requiem, yet they are in truth the meritorious members of the republic, and too often their services go unrewarded, and their memory is suffered to rot beneath the polluted touch of some designing biographer.

Rev. H. H. Spalding is the sole survivor of the heroic band who crossed the continent in 1836 under the auspices of the Board of Foreign Missions of the New School Presbyterian Church.   He feels keenly the wrong that has been done him and those whose memory he cherishes.

The members of our congressional delegation will be earnestly memorialized to secure some action of Congress that will place on record a refutation of the slander that has been permitted to go forth under its seal and sanction.   The highest ecclesiastical authority of every Protestant denomination in the State either has or will soon add their voices against the prejudicial statements of the priest Brouilette, who evidently wrote in the most malicious spirit.   As to J. Ross Browne, he richly deserves to be held up to the scorn and contempt of every honest man for suffering himself to be made the mouth-piece for trumpeting forth a gross and malicious calumny against the most self-sacrificing band of Christian pioneers that ever braved the dangers of a pagan wilderness.

Doc. F.—Report of the Committee on Protestantism in Oregon.

The committee of investigation in relation to Protestantism in Oregon, as set forth in Executive Document No. 38 of the Thirty-fifth Congress of the United States, House of Representatives, would respectfully report:

That they have, as far as circumstances would permit, carefully examined the subject committed to them in connection with said document, and find that in 1857 the Commissioner of Indian Affairs and the Treasury Department of Washington appointed J. Ross Browne a special agent on the subject of the Indian war in Oregon, which began in the massacre by the Indians of Dr. Marcus Whitman, his wife, and 18 others, in the fall of 1847; that in pursuance of the object of his appointment said J. Ross Browne prepared and transmitted a report to the Commissioner of Indian Affairs.   That said report comprehends 66 pages of said congressional document, while but 12 pages are composed of matter prepared by said Browne; the remainder, 54 pages, consisting of what was first published in a Roman Catholic newspaper in New York City, and afterward issued as a pamphlet, and sent to the world, over the signature of a Jesuit priest by the name of Brouilette.   This pamphlet, constituting so large a part of Browne's report and sent abroad over the land, purports to give a true history of the missions under the patronage of the American Board on this coast, which were broken up and destroyed by the massacre above mentioned.

The object of Brouilette's pamphlet appears to be to exculpate the real instigators of that terrible tragedy, and cast the blame upon the Protestant missionaries themselves, who were the victims of the bloody affray.

Your committee believe themselves possessed of the most abundant testimony, both from civil and military officers of the United States, and from many other citizens of the most reliable credibility, that the portion of Browne's report for which he is indebted to the Jesuit priest is full of the most glaring and infamous falsehoods, which renders it unworthy the confidence of every man, and is artfully calculated to mislead the public mind in regard to the whole transaction, and to cast the most unjust and cruel reflections upon the characters of those devoted missionaries of the American Board, who were faithfully laboring at that time among the Caynses at Waiilatpu, and the Nez Perces.

If the above-named paper had been published simply upon individual responsibility, there would, even then, have been some occasion for the lovers of truth and justice to takes measures to destroy its influence; but in this case the shameful libel has been sent abroad by the authority of the Congress of the United States, and the truth of history, as well as the character of the insulted and injured, demands of all those who have any knowledge of the facts a full and thorough vindication.

It was in 1834 that a Christian church of the United States sought first to introduce into the Territory of Oregon (a title then applied to all our Pacific domain north of California) Christianity and the arts of civilized life.   At that time unbroken heathenism prevailed throughout this vast country; but in September of that year four Christian men, wearied and weather-beaten by thousands of miles of journeying over trackless wilds, might have been seen erecting their tents on the banks of the beautiful Willamette, and with their Bibles, their hymn-books, and their axes, striking the first blows for Christianity and civilization on the great Pacific slope.   In any exhibition of historic truth in relation to religion and civilization on the Pacific shores, the names of the intrepid Jason Lee and his companions must always hold the most important place.   Thus commencing the work, we find that six years afterward there had a company of missionaries collected in Lower or Western Oregon, under the patronage of the Board of Missions of the Methodist Episcopal Church, of 67 persons, a number nearly equal to that of the Pilgrims who landed on Plymouth Rock, just 249 years before, and laid the foundations of a mighty empire.

The Lees were followed in 1837 by Messrs. Whitman, Spalding, and Gray, and soon after by Rev. Messrs. Walker, and Elles, and others, accompanied by teachers, farmers, mechanics, a printer, and a physician.   With this company were the first white ladies, Mrs. Marcus Whitman and Mrs. H. H. Spalding, that ever crossed the Rocky Mountains.   This Christian colony, numbering but little less than twenty persons, were under the patronage of the American Board of Commissioners for Foreign Missions, and were all well qualified to promote the sole object for which they had left all the enjoyments and protection of civilized life, the introduction of Christian civilization among the savages of the interior of Oregon.

And thus in respect to both the colonies described, and without any express understanding on the subject, the missionaries themselves came to be the best agents of the Government in promoting the population of the country.

We find that the latter company of missionaries established themselves among the savages at different points in the interior, Dr. Marcus Whitman on the Walla-Walla at Waiilatpu, Rev. H. H. Spalding at Lapwai on the Clear Water, and the remainder at points in the valley of the great Columbia, where their labors were most needed. Applying themselves with great diligence and constancy to their work, it was soon apparent that their laborious, trying, and self-denying exertions in behalf of the red man were not in vain.   A knowledge of agriculture and the mechanic arts had been acquired by many of them, and by the untiring assiduity of Mr. and Mrs. Spalding the Indian language had been reduced to a system, and books to some extent had been put into their hands, and education and religion were exerting their benign influence, softening the savage disposition, and moulding and elevating their character.

Thus these indefatigable missionaries labored on for eleven long years, witnessing the ripening fruits already resulting from their efforts, in the rapid progress which the objects of their love and solicitude were making in almost everything pertaining to modern civilization; and all this, notwithstanding the subtle and unrelenting hostility which they had to encounter from the enemies of American interests in the country, but especially from the Jesuit emissaries of Rome.   This opposition became more and more apparent as the evidences of the success of the missionaries became more and more manifest and satisfactory, till at length, in the fall of 1847, it culminated in one of the most fearful and horrid tragedies that the human mind can possibly imagine. Dr. Whitman, whose every energy had been consecrated to the elevation and wellbeing of the Indian race, his accomplished wife, who hesitated not to exchange the luxuries of wealth and refinement for exposure and toil and suffering in a heathen land, and eighteen other persons, while in the midst of fancied security, were butchered in cold blood. Women whose husbands lay weltering in gore, and young ladies whose brothers had fallen victims to savage barbarity, were dragged away from the bleeding and lifeless forms of their friends and subjected to a fate even worse than death itself; and many children were taken into captivity, where they remained until they were relieved by ransom. This terrible tragedy occurred at Waiilatpu, on the Walla-Walla River, and the facts pertaining to it, which are fully attested by an array of evidence sufficient to place them beyond the possibility of a doubt, all go to prove the following points:

1. That the massacre was wholly unprovoked by Dr. Whitman, or any other member or members of the mission; while, on the other hand, the victims themselves were employed at the very time they were attacked in relieving the sufferings of the Indians arising from the prevalence of an epidemical disorder of unusual fatality.

II. That the true causes of the massacre may be found in the policy and course pursued by the Hudson's Bay Company, which was an embodiment of the British government at that time in the country, to exclude American settlers from the land, and the efforts of Roman priests directed against the establishment of Protestantism in the country, which they hoped to accomplish by preventing its settlement by American citizens. These two things, a knowledge of which was possessed by the savages, operated upon their dark, suspicious minds, and excited them, doubtlessly, to perpetrate the horrid butchery, and to inflict upon the survivors the most indescribable brutalities.

III. That the objects sought by these atrocities were as above stated appears very clear, from the fact that immigrants on their way to the lower country, then resting a season at the premises, shared the same fate that fell upon the missionaries. Furthermore, the massacre was entirely confined to American Protestants; the Catholics on and about the premises walked unhurt amidst the slaughter, and Brouilette himself came to the spot before the ground had drank the blood of the victims, and while yet the mangled bodies remained unburied, baptized the Indians amidst the general desolation which his own machinations had contributed to effect.

IV. It also appears very clear by the accumulated testimony in the case, that not only was the mission at Waiilatpu broken up and destroyed by the massacre, but all the Protestant missionaries among the Nez Perces and other tribes of the interior were compelled, from the same cause, to abandon their different fields, while the missionaries of the Roman Church remained in perfect security among the tribes, and in the immediate vicinity of the scenes of blood and carnage already described. These astounding atrocities being made public, and the evidence of their true origin becoming more and more apparent, it was natural for the instigators of the horrid crime to endeavor to exculpate themselves; and, in order to do this, they must fasten it upon some other persons, and hence the publication of the pamphlet alluded to, in which the author in every possible way attempts to stigmatize and traduce the character of Whitman and Spalding, and their heroic, devoted and estimable wives, whose noble deeds of Christian patriotism entitle them to the lasting gratitude of the entire country.

It now appears quite certain, by the testimony which has come to hand, that Browne himself, as well as Brouilette, wrote in the interests of the Roman Church, for on this ground only can it appear at all reasonable that he would have incorporated into his report so false a production as that of which it is affirmed in the Congressional document under consideration, that "it will form an interesting and authentic chapter in the history of the Protestant missions." In this character, Browne, acting on the principle that lies at the basis of all Jesuitical ethics, that "the end justifies the means," took advantage of his position as an officer of the Government to advance the interests of Romanism by covering with obloquy the memory of those who sacrificed their lives for the promotion of republican liberty and Christian civilization; and of utterly destroying the character of the only survivor of the heroic band who constituted the second section of the vanguard of civilization, and who were the first to plant the seeds of pure Christianity in eastern Oregon. We here refer to Rev. H. H. Spalding, whose arduous and long-continued labors, with those of his devoted wife, resulted in securing the fidelity of the Nez Perces, the most powerful tribe of Indians on the western slope, to American interests, so that in all the Indian wars which have followed the Whitman massacre, they have, with few exceptions, always remained true, and by their influence and power have often prevented the desolations of savage warfare from sweeping over the white settlements of the country. Under the teachings of these devoted servants of the red race, the Nez Perces were so bound to American interests and to Protestant Christianity that no hostile tribes nor Roman emissaries have ever been able to draw them away from their friendship and allegiance; and though, by the unwise policy of Government officials, they have been deprived of the presence and council of their beloved missionary for many long years, yet most of them still stand firm in their religion, and remain the most uncompromising friends of the American people.

With these facts before us, we would unite with all lovers of truth and justice in earnestly petitioning the Congress of the United States, as far as possible, to rectify the evils which have resulted from the publication as a congressional document of the slanders of J. Ross Browne; and thus lift the cloud of darkness that hangs over the memory of the righteous dead, and extend equal justice to those who survive.

C. KINGSLEY,
Moderator.
GUSTAVUS HINES,
I. D. DRIVER,
A. F. WALLER,
JOHN SPENCER,
H. K. HINES,
J. H. WILBUR,
Members of the Committee.

Resolutions of the Oregon presbytery of the Cumberland Presbyterian Church.

1. Whereas a pamphlet has recently appeared in our midst entitled "Protestantism in Oregon," published by one J. B. A. Brouilette, a priest of the sect of Rome, dated at New York, 1853, and purporting to contain a detailed account of the Whitman massacre and its causes.

2. And whereas the said pamphlet contains many statements reflecting great discredit upon the early Protestant missionaries in Oregon, and particularly upon the lamented Dr. Whitman, Rev. H. H. Spalding, and their sainted wives.

3. And whereas it is attempted to be shown, in said pamphlet, that the massacre of the Whitman family and others was the result of the improper bearing of Dr. Whitman and Rev. H. H. Spalding among the Indians.

4. And whereas, to our astonishment, we find said pamphlet published in Ex. Doc. No. 38, Thirty-fifth Congress, 1st session, House of Representatives, accompanying a letter from J. Ross Browne, special agent of Treasury Department, to the Commissioner of Indian Affairs, dated at San Francisco, December 4, 1857.

Now, therefore, it is resolved by this presbytery:

1st. That it is the opinion of this presbytery, from a multitude of most reliable testimony now before us on the subject, that the unfavorable statements, made in the pamphlet referred to in the preceding preamble, concerning the early Protestant missionaries in Oregon, are in the highest degree false and slanderous.

2d. That this presbytery regards it not only as a duty, but as an esteemed privilege, to express her confidence in the character of the late Dr. Marcus Whitman, possessing, in a large degree, the elements of a true Christian character, and native goodness of heart, and purity of life. And that to his labors, more than to any other one man, we are indebted for preventing what is now the State of Oregon and Territory of Washington from falling into the hands of the British Government To render which service to our Government and the cause of Protestantism Dr. Whitman performed a journey across the continent in midwinter.

3d. That what has been said of the merits of Dr. Whitman, as a man and a Christian of high moral worth, is affirmed; also, and with equal pleasure, of Rev. H. H. Spalding, who, in the order of a kind Providence, is now spending the evening of his life in our midst, happily surrounded by his children and his children's children.

And further, it affords us great pleasure to indorse what has been often affirmed by others, that Rev. H. H. Spalding and his amiable and accomplished wife, now in heaven, have done more through their labors, as missionaries, to civilize and Christianize the Nez Perces tribe of Indians than the Government has ever been able to accomplish by an outlay of vast sums of money. And further, that to their influence is mainly attributed the steadfast friendship of the Nez Perces, under all circumstances, to the white population, even when all the surrounding tribes—under Roman influence—were at war with the American people.

4th. That, from what is regarded as evidence of the most reliable character, this presbytery is fully convinced that the Roman clergy, then occupying the country, were the principal instigators of the Whitman tragedy.

W. R. BISHOP, *Moderator.*
C. A. WOOLEY, *Clerk.*

Doc. C.—*Resolutions adopted by the Congregational Association of Oregon at the meeting in Salem, June, 1869.*

Your committee, to whom was referred Executive Document No. 38, of the Thirty-fifth Congress, first session, House of Representatives, respectfully report:

That they have carefully examined said document, and to their surprise find that (while published under the authority of the Congress of the United States, as though a report of J. Ross Browne) it contains only twelve pages of matter prepared by said Browne, and fifty-three other pages, consisting of matter first published in a Roman

Catholic newspaper in New York city, and afterward issued as a pamphlet prepared by a Jesuit priest by the name of Brouilette.   This pamphlet purports to give a true account of the Protestant missions involved in the Indian massacre of 1847, in which Dr. Whitman and nineteen others lost their lives, and the missions were broken up.

Your committee find from overwhelming evidence, from the testimony of different United States officers, civil and military, and from other citizens of most reliable credibility, that this portion of said congressional document involved in it so many prominent and absolute falsehoods as to give a most erroneous impression to the whole, and to cast most fallacious and infamous reflections upon the characters of the devoted and faithful missionaries of the American Board there laboring at that time.

It positively appears that this Jesuit priest (Brouilette) was, as he himself admits, present among the Indians at the time of the massacre, and at the very place, and was actually baptizing the children of the murdering Indians while the outrage was going on, and in the presence of unburied bodies of the victims, and in hearing of the screams of the suffering prisoners.   That Roman Catholic priests did carry arms and ammunition to the hostile Indians, and that when Captain Rogers intercepted this ammunition at the Dalles the priests did vigorously threaten that all the Catholic Indian tribes, French and Hudson's Bay men would attack the little garrison and settlements if he dared to take the arms and ammunition.

Your committee believe, from evidence clear and sufficient to them, that the Roman Catholic priests did themselves instigate violence to the missions resulting in the massacre; and that this pamphlet, so most strangely published by Congress, with no rebutting statements accompanying it, was prepared by them to throw the blame of the massacre upon the American missionaries.

Your committee conclude by presenting for your adoption the following resolutions:

Resolved, That as members of the Congregational Association of Oregon, and long acquainted with the surviving members of the Oregon Mission of the American Board, we believe them to have been, and to be, persons of veracity and of sincere Christian devotion and of unquestionable benevolence in their labors to civilize and Christianize the Indian tribes.

Resolved, That their labors redounded immensely to the promotion of all American interests on this coast, if not indeed to the preservation of the country to the American Union.

Resolved, That we learn with great satisfaction that the Rev. H. H. Spalding has collected authentic documents for a truthful history of the whole matter, conclusively refuting the foul statements of the Jesuits.

Resolved, That we respectfully ask of Congress that, as this erroneous pamphlet of a foreign emissary of the Pope of Rome has, under their sanction, been given to the world, so a candid and truthful account of the matter thus treated of, which is now being prepared by an able committee of reliable American citizens, may also be published under their sanction in a like congressional document.

Resolved, That from acquaintance with facts for the last twenty years, and other clear evidence, we believe that the missionaries, contrary to the statements made by Congress, did not abandon the mission at Lapwai, but were first forced away by the war, and that those who have since been anxious to return have been steadily excluded by Government officials, even to having their houses pulled down, and the agents of the board threatened with violence if they persisted.

O. DICKENSON,
I. V. BLAKESLEE,
ELKANAH WALKER, Committee.
G. H. ATKINSON,
Moderator of Oregon Association.

Attest: CHESTER N. TERRY,
Clerk of Congregational Association of Oregon.

DOC. D.—*Resolutions adopted by the Oregon Presbytery of the United Presbyterian Church at their meeting in Linn County, in 1868 and 1869.*

We, the ministers and ruling elders of the Oregon Presbytery of the United Presbyterian Church, some of us being residents of Oregon at the time of the Whitman massacre, agree upon the following expressions of opinion, to wit:

1st. Dr. Marcus Whitman and wife, and Rev. H. H. Spalding and wife, for their Christian zeal, devotedness, and unyielding perseverance through fearful hazards and long-continued hardships for months during their journey over the Rocky Mountains, across the continent, on horseback and without bread, where the foot of white woman had never trod, to establish the kingdom of truth, and plant the tree of civilization on these then dark shores of paganism, amid privations of self denial most fearful; 3,000 miles from home and friends, and where no succor could reach them, other than that invoked from the God they worshiped, are entitled to the respect, esteem, love and sympathy, both in regard to those yet living and the memory of the dead, of the entire Christian church, in all its various denominations. not only in Oregon, but throughout the whole world.

2d. The tribes among whom they located in 1836 were in a state of entire wildness and savageism, starving on a meager supply of roots, fish and game; not a foot of land in cultivation; not a hoe, plow or cow; without a knowledge of letters, of the Sabbath, or human salvation.

3d. That this wild wilderness should so soon be changed, "the desert to bud and blossom," the fields to wave with grain—from 15,000 to 2),000 bushels of grain harvested yearly by the Nez Perces tribe, among whom Mr. Spalding and his amiable wife located; orchards and gardens planted, cattle roaming in bands, schools established, in which from 100 to 500 souls were in daily attendance, women spinning and weaving, over 100 adoring the Christian faith, churches organized, family altars erected, the language reduced to a written state, portions of God's word translated and printed—the only instance on the Pacific coast—speak volumes for the fidelity and efficiency of those faithful servants of Jesus Christ, and evince the presence of God's Spirit among them, while it places them, in the minds of every candid thinker, above the imputation of being influenced by low, selfish, and worldly motives.

4th. As proof of the above we might refer to the present superior intelligence, enterprise, and good order which distinguished the Nez Perces tribe from the surrounding tribes; as also to a great amount of testimony now before us from George Abernathy, esq., then governor of the Territory of Oregon; from Commodore Wilks, an eye-witness in 1841; from Rev. G. Hines, in 1843; from General Joel Palmer, in 1846, 1847, and 1848; from Colonels Steptoe, Alvord, Cornelius, Agent Anderson, Governor Daniels, and scores of our citizens, civil and military officers, miners and travelers of most reliable character, all bear uniform testimony to the above declarations.

5th. The strong alliance and unwavering friendship of the Nez Perces to the Americans, while all the surrounding tribes have been at times hostile and repeatedly in arms against the United States; and when, in 1848, had they joined the combined tribes under the Roman priests, the last American family on this coast would have been cut off, as testifies Governor Abernathy before the committee. And when again, in 1856, all the tribes on this Northwest coast were combined against the Americans, except the Nez Perces. as testifies Colonel Cornelius to the same committee, under the priests, had the Nez Perces joined them, if the American settlements had not been annihilated they would have been involved in a most disastrous and expensive war—their constant friendship being fairly, by abundant testimony before us, attributable to the instructions and influence of Mr. Spalding and his sainted wife, now in heaven—render them worthy the most favorable considerations of the American Government, rather than the foul and libelous slanders which they are sending forth to the world in their executive documents.

6th. In demonstrating the practicability of an overland route connecting the eastern and western slopes of the North American continent for families, herds, and wagons, Mrs. Spalding and Mrs. Whitman being the first white women who, in obedience to their Lord, had the Christian courage to turn their backs upon weeping parents and the civilized world, and face the hazards and unknown dangers of this then great and terrible wilderness, where so many stout men had perished, and pronounced impossible for a white woman. In the encouragement and aid given by them to the weary, way-worn emigrants to this western wilderness, in the influence they exerted in sustaining the just claims of our Government to the vast field embraced in the dispute, and thereby thwarting the schemes of intriguing European diplomatists, these pioneer missionaries, both overland and by sea, are entitled to gratitude from every American citizen.

7th. It is our deliberate conviction that the Lapwai mission belongs to the American Board of Commissioners for Foreign Missions, as the mission home of our Brother Spalding. 1st. By the lawful permit of the American Government now before us, dated War Department, March, 1836, for the said board, in the person of Rev. H. H. Spalding and family, to enter and settle in said Nez Perces country as a teacher and missionary. 2d. By contract of said tribe in council, November, 1836. 3d. By eleven years' residence, and until forced away. 4th. By the acts of Congress in 1848, and in 1852, both of which confirm the title of the land to the American Board. And we heartily concur in the opinions set forth by his excellency Governor Abernathy, by General Palmer, by Colonel Cornelius, and by some 600 of the best citizens of our State, in a memorial to our government praying that they may be allowed to renew the work of Protestant missions at the old Lapwai station, which prayer, though renewed for three years, has been steadily refused. That the interests of the Government and of the tribe would be better subserved by the appointment of Mr. Spalding there than by any other man.

8th. We heartily concur in the above named memorial, in which every religious body in the State has concurred so far as there has been opportunity, as also the citizens of Oregon and Washington, numbering 600 or more, irrespective of party or religious sects, including the very best citizens and most of the officers, civil and military, both of the present date and of former years, to wit: Mr. Anderson, for several years agent of the Nez Perces, does not, in our opinion, exaggerate in saying that the friendly relations always maintained by the Nez Perces with the Americans is in a great measure to be attributed to the teachings of Mr. Spalding, and that in his opinion Mr. Spalding, by his own personal labors, has accomplished more good to this tribe than all the money expended by Government has been able to effect.

9th. The plea of voluntary abandonment of the Lapwai mission December, 1847, by the missionaries, as put forth by the Thirty-seventh Congress, is simply absurd. Oregon history of that date, and the testimony of the governor, the officers of the Army, and most of the citizens, show conclusively that Mrs. Spalding, the only missionary at Lapwai at that date, being one of eight days of the bloody carnage, her husband and daughter supposed to be among the slain, and her three infant children were barely delivered from the tomahawk of the savage Indians, by her faithful Nez Perces, and taken that 4th of December, 1847, to a point of safety in the timber. This is called by a Christian Congress "voluntary abandonment;" and that after Mr. Spalding was brought in, more dead than alive, from lacerated bare feet on ice, and prickly pear, cut rocks, freezing, want of sleep, and starving six days and nights, himself and family; the other fifty-two women and children prisoners, including the last American in the country, were redeemed by P. S. Ogden, of the Hudson's Bay Company, by paying the Indians $1,000; were taken out of the country. the long wars commenced, and the country was closed by Government against *all missionaries*, and remained closed till 1858. And it is well known and proved that so soon as it was thought safe Brother Spalding attempted to return, but was forbidden, and that when he did and opened his schools among his old people, who were rejoiced to see him, and at once filled up church and school-room, as testified by Agent Anderson, these were broken up and himself forced from his old home, his orchards, buildings, his people and his native church, of nearly thirty years' pastorate, by Government officials.

10th. We are decided in our convictions that the Nez Perces are the people among whom Mr. Spalding, as missionary and minister, should be allowed to labor. His long residence, his perfect knowledge of their language—no other person can preach it—the mutual attachment existing between himself and them; their strong and oft-repeated desire for his return; his unquenchable ardor to labor and die among them; his former great, perhaps unparalleled success, together with other kindred qualifications, eminently fit him for missionary service among that people. The heroic courage of himself and wife displayed through that long, most hazardous and tedious journey to reach their field of labor; their great service to their country; the sacred associations of the place, being the birth-place of all his children, and where he and his companion spent the best part of their lives, and where they often witnessed the display of God's converting grace, consecrating that land to Christ and to liberty with their prayers, their sweat, and their blood, all present Brother Spalding's claim to the Lapwai mission as morally just and beyond dispute.

11th. We believe it was through the efforts of the early missionaries to this country that it was thrown open to and settled by the citizens of the United States, and that in a special degree are we indebted to the late martyred Whitman, whose presence in Washington City in March, 1843, through severe winter sufferings, very opportunely prevented the consummation of a transfer of Oregon to England.

12th. From personal knowledge and overwhelming testimony, we are convinced that Romanism and British influence were the main causes of the Whitman massacre, the wars that followed, the prosecuting and banishing from the country the Protestant missionaries, destroying their property and imperiling their health and lives. Romanism has, we are persuaded, with a bitterness unparalleled except in the past history of its own bloody acts, attempted, in every way possible to them, the utter subversion of Protestantism in Oregon.

13th. From our knowledge of Ex-Governor Abernathy, General Palmer, and Hon. A. Hinman, we say without hesitation that we believe them to be men of integrity and veracity, above suspicion, and that consequently the testimony collected from them by Rev. H. H. Spalding may be implicitly relied upon.

While Romanism in its senility is showing signs of its speedy dissolution, we unite in sympathy with Brother Spalding and all other Protestants throughout the land who are now or who have been suffering under their unhallowed influence. We heartily unite with them before God's bar in prayer, that the days of the man of sin may soon be numbered.

JAMES DICK,
Moderator of Presbytery.

T. S. KENDALL,
    Clerk of Presbytery.

T. S. KENDALL,
J. McCOY,
Committee.

[Resolutions similar to the above were passed by the Cumberland Presbytery and by the Congregational Association of Oregon.]

Doc. G.—Resolutions adopted by the Pleasant Butte Baptist Church of Linn County, Oregon, October 22, 1869.

Whereas our American Congress have, with apparent good intentions and with all earnestness, felt themselves called upon to undertake the censorship of the Protestant Church; and whereas they have published by their vote and sanction a pamphlet entitled "Executive Document No. 38, House of Representatives, Thirty-fifth Congress, first session," thus giving to it the authority and sanction both of the House of Representatives and the Executive.

This executive document contains a report of the Hon. J. Ross Browne, special agent of the Government to the Pacific coast, and founded, as Browne says, only "on reliable historical data."

But this so-called report of the agent, of 66 pages, with the exception of a short preface of 12 pages by the agent, was written years before by a Jesuit from the Pacific coast, and published in a Romish newpaper in New York, and appears now in this "executive document," word for word, constituting the report of Browne and receiving the sanction of Congress.

This document, under the remarkable heading "Protestantism in Oregon," contains this significant language: "These pages will form an interesting and authentic chapter in the history of Protestant missions."

This congressional "chapter" on "Protestant missions" purports to give a record of the testimony and the trial of "Protestantism in Oregon," in the persons of four of Oregon's early pioneers and missionaries, for very high crimes and misdemeanors, and among them the highest crimes known to mortals, that of high treason against the Captain of human salvation, by assuming the character of Christian teachers before the Christian Church, obtaining their funds, making great pledges to the natives of yearly ships loaded with goods to be given, not sold, to the Indians, of great sums for their lands, but steadily breaking all these pledges, refusing to give or pay the price fixed, or to teach or to aid the Indians to anything "unless paid a high price," but "persisted to stay" and proceeded to rob the natives of "their horses, cattle, and grain;" "imported poison from the States" to "poison the Indians" to "obtain their spotted horses and lands;" incited massacres and wars with a view "to exterminate the settlements;" and alongside of these crimes is given in this executive document a catalogue of the virtues and glowing deeds of Romanism in Oregon among the natives, and in their multiplied labors to aid the early American settlements, and especially their timely and self-sacrificing efforts, even "at the risk of their lives," to stay the bloody massacre invoked at Waiilatpu by the Protestant missionaries, and to deliver the missionaries and to "redeem the captive American women and children."

And thus, in offering this executive document as a chapter on Protestant missions, Congress has felt constrained to throw down the gauntlet and have fairly forced upon us, Protestants of Oregon, the challenge to compare the record of "Protestantism in Oregon" with the record of "Romanism in Oregon:" Therefore,

Resolved, As Oregonians and as Protestants, we accept the challenge, with all deference to our Executive and the House of Representatives, and proceed at once to the comparison by reviewing the records of both Protestantism and of Romanism in Oregon; and in doing so we shall also rely "only upon reliable historic data," a history known and read of all men, and written upon the ground, and not in the dark cells of New York, 3,000 miles away, and with hands at the moment dripping with the blood of Protestants and of American mothers and infants, butchered by their instigation.

2. *Resolved*, That we reject, with unutterable mortification as Americans, and deep detestation as Protestants, this chapter on Protestant missions, which our American Congress has prepared at such great labor, and sent forth at public expense, on the wheels of the Post Office Department, and for the following reasons, to wit:

I. Because it breathes the most malignant bitterness against the Protestant Church, and was manifestly published for the benefit of the Romish hierarchy, and to exculpate a band of the most atrocious butchers of American fathers, mothers, and infants, and designed, whether by Congress or not, certainly by Rome, as a club in the hands of Congress against Protantism.

II. Because it is a libel on Oregon's history and a gross and most malicious calumny against the most self-sacrificing band of patriots and Christian pioneers that ever braved the dangers of a pagan wilderness.

III. Because that, from personal knowledge, some of us being in the country at the time, and from a vast array of testimony now before us, from old Oregonians, from eye-witnesses, from the captives, from military and civil officers, we are convinced that it was the Romish clergy and British agents who instigated the Whitman massacre, in which Dr. Whitman, his amiable wife, Mrs. Spalding, and seventeen others, mostly American emigrants stopping to winter and recruit, lost their lives, and the most brutal atrocities practiced upon female captives reserved for a fate worse than death, the Protestant missions broken up, the last American forced to leave Middle Oregon, and the country involved in the long and most disastrous Indian wars.

IV. Because the "executive document," or so-called chapter on Protestant mission, was written by one of the principal instigators of that most horrible butchery, a Jesuit by the name of J. B. A. Brouilette, the vicar-general of the Pacific coast, and published in the Freeman's Journal, New York, a paper that has always proclained its hatred of Protestantism and our free schools and free press. From abundant testimony he, this vicar-general, was on the ground at Waiilatpu during the horrible butchery, which lasted eight days, with his bishop and thirteen priests, direct from Europe, camped at helping distance around, and with one of his overland party, an educated Indian from Canada, standing at the window by the doctor's head, to give the signal for the tomahawking to commence; who shot Mrs. Whitman through the breast, and with his own hands butchered Hoffman and two other Americans, and who told the Cayuses and Oregon Indians that he had seen, before he left the States, the letters of Mrs. Whitman and Mr. Spalding, calling for poison, to come by the emigrants, to kill the Cayuses and Nez Perces; that it was a question of life or death with them—they must destroy the Americans while few or be destroyed; he would help them, and the bishop and the vicar-general, who had just come over from the Pope, their great father, would furnish plenty of ammunition from the English post.

This Brouilette, to remove all doubt from the minds of the Oregon Indians as to his abhorrence of Americans, and as *pay down* for butchering the heretics, actually proceeded to baptize the blood-stained children of the butchering savages, while the butchery was going on and the unburied dead and gasping bodies lay about his feet, hogs and dogs running about with parts in their mouths, the screams of our ever-to-be-pitied young women, writhing in the hands of unrestrained brutality, his church-music; and who, with his bishop and associates, handed over with their own hands our young, helpless girls to be brutalized before their eyes, and turned our escaped fathers and infants and mothers out of doors, to be scalped by the savages; and who, when our dear, helpless children and mothers were huddled in a corner, with blood-streaming tomahawks brandished over their heads by the Indian women, crying to the chiefs, "Shall we strike?" rushed in among them and took a phial from the doctor's shelf, holding it up to the excited Indians, cried out through his Canadian helper, "Here is the identical poison; see what your Protestants Whitman and Spalding were doing; bury this or you are all dead;" and all this to excite the savages to chop our helpless children and mothers to pieces on the spot.

And who after all this—the last Protestant missionary and American killed or forced out of Eastern Oregon, but his hellish hate of Protestantism and Americans not yet sufficiently gloated—could meditate the horrible butchery and the attendant atrocities of the entire American settlements, and for that purpose shipped up the river from the English post at Vancouver over four thousand pounds of powder and balls, and boxes of guns for the combined savages, and which were taken from them by Lieutenant Rogers and his little band of faithful Protestants only fifteen miles short of the camp at Des Chutes, who had boasted only three days before that plenty of ammunition was coming up by the priests, and then they "would come down and scalp Americans and take their women and cattle."

And these are the Jesuit monsters whose record in Oregon is thus written with Protestant blood and the blood of American fathers, and infants, and mothers, who receive by vote of the American Congress the copyright to prepare testimony against and chapters on Protestant missions, and our House of Representatives are compelled to resolve themselves into a publishing-house to publish the same, and the Army officers into a corps of colporteurs to circulate them.

The Brouilette, who could thus help on this horrid butchery of Protestants and Americans, could thus revel in female anguish and the screams of scalped infants, could thus refuse help to agonized mothers, and could, in cool blood, meditate the butchery of the last American family on this coast, not able to meet the overwhelming testimony against him, published at the time on the spot, and fearing the just indignation of the Americans, fled three thousand miles to New York, and, safe in the cells of New York inquisition, prepared this paper, composed of forgeries against the best citizens of Oregon, and the most revolting falsehoods against the memory of the unfortunate victims he had caused to be butchered, and all to exculpate their guilty heads. And while it remained a Romish production by such monsters, no one took any notice of it, but, to our utter astonishment, it now appears, word for word, in this executive document, and is offered to us by the American Congress, with an audacity that has no parallel in modern history, as "an interesting and authentic chapter in the history of Protestant missions;" but we reject it with becoming American disdain, and as Protestants of this Pacific West we respectfully advise Congress to burn it, to call in every document without delay and burn them. You owe it to yourselves, to your country, and to the age. And,

V. We reject this chapter or record of the court—if trial it is to be regarded, and such it will be by a majority of readers—because of the irregular and extraordinary mode of getting it up; and—

1. The so-called court had no jurisdiction in the case. The American Congress is not

an ecclesiastical body, not even a judicial; but the case is purely religious, being Protestantism in Oregon.

2. It had no jurisdiction as to territory. The fourscore and ten crimes as found in the bill of indictment, made out in the walls of the New York inquisition, are set forth as committed in Oregon Territory, but the court sits in the city of Washington, three thousand miles away, thus repeating in this republican commonwealth the fearful crimes loudest complained of by the fathers of 1776.

3. Three of the four individuals brought before the court for trial were dead, and had been for years; fell martyrs to that very Government which is thus tearing open their graves secretly in Oregon and taking their characters off three thousand miles to Washington to blacken them in their public documents; and the only survivor not notified of said intended trial (another breach of the Constitution) consequently had no opportunity to confront testimony or to offer testimony, when more than property or life was at stake, (another breach of the Constitution) and the court, even the Congress of the United States, refuses to appoint a counsel, which is done in every court of the civilized world, even for the vilest of criminals, showing the deadly prejudice and bitterness of the court against the criminal, Protestantism.

4. There was no jury. Thus, in seven particulars, the fundamental principles of the sacred Constitution of the United States are grossly violated in this royal farce.

5. The character of the testimony which Congress thought all-sufficient in this trial of "Protestantism in Oregon," and the manner of collecting it, caps the climax. Nothing like it in the history of any court in the civilized world, and fit rather for the dark ages of the Spanish inquisition. Much is forgery outright; for instance, that of General Joel Palmer and honorable Robert Newell is proved to be such by the testimony of those gentlemen before our committee. By the testimony of these gentlemen nine forgeries are detected (perhaps there are ninety nine) in this royal chapter, declared under the official and sacred oath of this dignified body to be "founded only on reliable historical data."

But the manner of collecting the testimony. Not a witness is sworn or even called before the court, either in Washington or this country, and not required to state what they knew, but simply what they had heard second, fourth, and in some instances, eight-handed.

It seems that this Browne was dignified by the title of special agent of the Treasury Department, as a blind, whereas his real business appears to have been to collect absurdities and the grossest falsehoods against Protestantism, who straightway passed secretly through Oregon without giving the least idea that he was collecting testimony with which to enable Congress to try those Protestant women, Mrs. Spalding and Mrs. Whitman, for the crime of crossing the Rocky Mountains and the continent three thousand miles, and of robbing four large tribes of Indians of their horses, their cattle, and grain, and lands, and then poisoning them all, with the help only of their husbands, and passed on to the walls of the New York inquisition and found his brother Jesuit Browne, who employed him at once, entered upon the office of subcontractor to collect testimony, and brought out his paper to be received and declared by Congress to be "reliable historical data," with the understanding that no oath should be required, as almost every word was either forgery upon old Oregonians, or the falsehoods and reported sayings of the savages who had been executed, why they undertook to exterminate the Americans. Fifteen of the so-called witnesses in this strange document are known to have been concerned in that bloody tragedy.

This whole thing is a disgrace to Congress, to the Executive, to the American people, and the highest possible insult to the Protestent church of the United States. Indeed, the most significant and most fearful feature of the whole affair is, not that the superstitious Indians could be made to kill their benefactors; not that Jesuits could excite savages to butcher the hated heretics, scalp American mothers and infants, and hand over with their own hands our young women to be brutalized before their eyes; not that the Roman priests could undertake to aid the savages by furnishing ammunition to burn the infant settlements, butcher its inhabitants, and subject the captive infants and mothers to a fate worse than death; but that this paper should be offerd by the American Congress, with its solemn sanction, and the seal of the Executive, to the Protestant church of these United States as "an interesting and authentic chapter in the history of Protestant mission." (See page 13.)

This action of Congress utters a language louder and plainer than words can speak, and the more especially since the Thirty-ninth Congress and its Executive have proclaimed in their document one of these faithful missionaries an apostate; that she abandoned her field voluntarily; that the American Board of Missions is no better than a band of thieves, and proceeded to sieze their mission lands in Idaho, and to drive the board, in the person of its attorney, off, by threatening, the title of which had been confirmed to that board by three acts of Government, the first bearing date March, 1836; and since the Thirty-ninth Congress and its Executive have proceeded to force the only survivor of these condemned missionaries, in his old age, the first resident clergyman on the Pacific coast, from his old home, secured to him by the above-named three acts of Government, made sacred by the oft displays of God's converting grace, and because the birthplace of all his children and the scene of the best part of his life and that of his companion, now in heaven, from his orchard, mills, and farm, from his beloved people, for whom he and his angel wife left the civilized world long years before the Government made footprints on this coast, and from his native church of nearly thirty-two years pastorate, and tore down his house and threw it into the river; and since the present Congress and Executive continue to keep forcible possession and to keep by force this old Protestant missionary from his work and his people, who have oft begged the President to allow their old pastor to return, and not to force Catholics upon them, and he as strongly desires to return and labor and die with them.

With the Rev. Mr. Spalding we are intimately acquainted. Here he has been longest and best known. He is our neighbor and brother, beloved in the church of Christ; and whereof we speak we know.

Protestantism in Oregon.

From the pages of Oregon's history, from the personal knowledge of some of us, having been residents of this Pacific coast for years, and from abundance of the most reliable testimony, we, the members of Pleasant Butte Baptist Church, agree upon the following expression of opinion:

It was, under God, Protestantism in Oregon which, after many strong efforts by Government, by John Jacob Astor, and by others, to establish American settlements on these Pacific shores, counted by Jefferson of the greatest national importance, had totally failed, did succeed, in the teeth of the most unrelenting and bloody opposition of Romanism and British influence, to establish the first successful and permanent American settlement on these vast shores, now so important a portion of our commonwealth.

1. By the crossing of the Rocky Mountains in 1834, (four years before any Romish priest set foot in Oregon,) by the Protestant Lee, the pioneer missionary, and his little band, to become permanent missionaries and settlers on this coast. And the undaunted patriotism exhibited by this Christian hero in his first interview with the governor of the Hudson's Bay Company, then a corrupt British monopoly on this coast. The governor said to Mr. Lee: "All needed supplies and facility in our power shall be afforded to your mission while you confine yourselves to your work as teachers, but the day you lay hands on beaver all supplies will be stopped, and you will be left destitute. The trade in furs and the commerce of these seas belong to us." The reply of the missionary, American withal, was prompt and characteristic: "Governor, it is true I was born a British subject; but I am now an American citizen, and as such I have and shall claim the same right on these shores as the most favored British subject, and that too by treaty. I shall therefore trade beaver where and when I please." The same reply, almost word for word, was made two years later to the same English officer, by that faithful Christian but stern patriot, Marcus Whitman. That determined the fate of both of these valuable men; they fell martyrs to this their country. The destruction of the one was brought about through apostate Americans and disaffected friends employed to misrepresent; that of the other by imported Romish agents and Hudson's Bay interpreters working upon the savages; but not till this great Pacific West was securely made a part of our national domain, and their enlightened, stern, American, unselfish patriotism claims for their memory the lasting gratitude of the nation rather than the malicious calumnies now being heaped upon them through Congress, evidently for the benefit of Romanism.

2. By the successful crossing of the continent in 1836, of those two Protestant women, Mrs. Spalding and Mrs. Whitman, emphatically the American heroines of the nineteenth century, the first women who, in obedience to the command of their Lord, had the Christian courage to turn their backs forever upon weeping friends and the civilized world, and to face the hazards of the Rocky Mountains and the vast unknown beyond, to be perhaps two years; to winter in the everlasting snows and dark defiles of the mountains; to do without bread, to ask their daily food of God, and receive it at the hands of hunters and from buffalo bands; liable every minute to be pounced upon by prowling bands, the party butchered or put afoot to starve; sick or well, compelled to travel on, where foot of woman never trod; the endurance of the horse to hold out the two years, and escape foes and starvation—their only hope where so many strong men had perished—new dangers and accumulating labors multiplying every hour upon their fainting bodies. An undertaking pronounced impossible for woman by every mountain-man, by George Catlin, and the missionary Lee. Mrs. Spalding, more dead than alive from starvation and the attendant horrible sufferings, the green buffalo causing fearful diarrhœa, when the Nez Perces, who had sent to the "rising sun" for the Book of God, met them, and gave her dried roots which served as bread. Thus did these two Protestant heroines, not for honor or for gold, but to seek God's benighted ones, over 3,000 miles from home, and where no succor could reach but that invoked from the God they trusted, by their own footsteps and personal hazards

settle the great national question that families, and herds, and wagons could scale the mountains and the sand deserts, and thus fairly establish the great emigrant route connecting the eastern and western slopes of the North American Continent, so soon replaced by the longest railroad and the greatest human work of the age. This emigrant route led to the settling of this great Pacific West by American settlements, and these again to the development of those vast gold fields so long hid from the eye of mortals, and the magic growth of this new half of our commonwealth. This endless amount of gold was manifestly decreed by the Almighty to be in time for our national debt and in part to speed the gospel wheels of salvation.

3. By the arrival in the valley of the Willamette, in 1837, by a journey of 22,000 miles around Cape Horn, of seven Protestant women, to be permanent residents with their husbands, and associates of the pioneer Lee, and who laid the foundation of civilized and Christian society in Western Oregon, and brought into existence, in 1841, the provisional government.

4. By the arrival in the years 1838, 1839, and 1840 of nine Protestant missionary ladies overland, and of 15 by sea, in all, on the 4th of July, 1841, 33 Protestant wives and mothers, with their husbands, six unmarried men and 29 children, 100 in all, (5 had died,) not as yet an emigrant mother in the country, (one had passed through to California,) to become permanent settlers, and to make these distant shores their future home for themselves and children, to roll back the thick darkness of unknown ages, to erect the standard of the cross, and plant a second North American Republic on these Pacific shores. Precisely the number of that noble band of pilgrims who landed on Plymouth rock, 22d of December, 1620, just 220 years before, whose record as the defenders of the true faith and the true fathers of this great American Republic is world-wide known and justly appreciated. And it is evident from our country's already Pacific possessions, that the record of the Atlantic mother will not suffer in the comparison with the Pacific daughter. Already the Protestant colony of 100 souls has become a half empire as in a day.

At twelve o'clock, on the 4th of July last, thirty-three years ago, two Protestant heroines, Mrs. Spalding and Mrs Whitman, alighted from their weary horses, themselves in great weakness, at the dividing point on the Rocky Mountains, in the famous South Pass, and after returning profound thanks to Almighty God for his heavenly care of them thus far, and dedicating themselves anew to his holy cause, with the banner of the cross in one hand and the stars and stripes in the other, they stepped down, the first American women, into the Territory of Oregon, and took formal possession in the name of their Saviour and their country, in the name of American mothers and of the American church; and being immediately confronted by the British lion, they instantly bearded the royal beast in his lair. Memorable day! It sealed the fate of Great Britain on these shores. Then, from the Spanish South to the Frozen North, with the exception of a few British trappers and traders, with Indian wives, it was an unbroken wilderness, brooded over by the darkness of ages unknown, without town or settlement, without school-house or church-going bell, except the new-begun mission on the Willamette of the pioneer Lee, and his three heroic brothers, without their wives. Every where this vast region was the undisputed home of the wild man and the wild beast, regarded even by our Government, on account of its rugged and wild nature, fit only for the savage, the beaver, and the gray bear. But what, in so short a time, has appeared? A half empire-born as in a day! Three great States, and their Senators in Congress. The whole vast region, from the Pacific waves to the mountain summit, mapped into territories, with their governments, and throughout the whole, springing into existence as by magic, are crowded cities and lively settlements, interlocked by the telegraph, the railroad and steamer, the daily stage and mail. In the thousand valleys and every mountain top of this great Pacific slope, the darkness and solitude of ages are displaced by the merry school, the hum of business, the temple, and the morning praises to the living God. Our numerous rivers and our vast Pacific shores, so lately the playground only of the sea otter, are white with a floating commerce, and from its numerous harbors vessels and steamers are daily leaving for the markets of New York and Liverpool, for China and Japan, laden with the abundant products of our rich valleys and vast prairies, the $60,000,000 of gold and silver a month from our snow-capped mountains.

And 5th. By securing from California in 1837, 600 head of cattle, in spite of the powerful opposition of the Hudson's Bay Company, through the efforts of the far-seeing Protestant, Lee. These cattle were divided among the mission, a few mountain men with Indian wives, according to funds invested, and became the foundation of the comfort and speedy wealth of the country, and effectually delivered the American settlement from the Hudson's Bay monopoly.

And 6th. By the arrival of the Protestant Whitman at the city of Washington, in March, 1843, through untold winter sufferings in the mountains of Utah and New Mexico, not an hour too soon to prevent the transfer of all Oregon to Great Britain to go into the Ashburton and Webster treaty for a codfishery on Newfoundland; by his personal representations to President Tyler of this country, of its vast importance, and his assurance of a wagon route, as he assured him we had taken cattle, a wagon, and his missionary families through six years before, and that he thus ventured his life through that wintry journey for the sole object of taking back a caravan of wagons through to the Columbia, and thus to settle the question forever that families and wagons could cross; this effectually committed the President and stopped the negotiations.

By his bringing successfully through to the Columbia, in spite of the combined and powerful influence of the Hudson's Bay Company, and Romanism, both at Washington and at Fort Hall, of that great emigration of 1843, with their two hundred wagons and herds, under the momentous conviction that, if he failed, Oregon was lost, as the Hudson's Bay Company had succeeded only the year before in suddenly planting a colony of 140 souls on the Pacific shores, from the Red River settlements by the Saskatchawan Pass. The news of their having passed the mountains caused a young priest, not thinking that an American was at the large table, to rise, and waving his hand, "Hurrah for Columbia! America is too late; we have got the country now." This astonishing but significant boast, coupled with the stopping of wagons at Fort Hall every year, aroused the patriot Whitman, who saw at a glance that not an hour could be lost, and, unsolicited and unrewarded, and even opposed by the tears of his wife and the entreaties of his associates, because of the almost certain death, leaving his home on the Walla-Walla in October, 1842, he undertook the herculean labor of reaching Washington through the terrific mountain snows of Utah and New Mexico that winter, to bring through a caravan of wagons. And again, on reaching Fort Hall that fall, coming up from important medical services in the rear of the long caravan, the good doctor found the head companies in great consternation and distress from the representations of the Hudson's Bay Company, that no wagons ever had nor ever could pass through the terrific Snake deserts and reach the Columbia, and confronting the British lion, as oft he had done, he stepped forward and said, "My countrymen, you have trusted me thus far; from this point I know the country; we took our families, cattle, and wagon through seven years ago, and these men know it. By the help of that kind Providence who has brought us thus far, we will reach the banks of the Columbia before the 20th of September." And the consequence was, that that large emigration passed successfully the Snake country and the Blue Mountains, under the guidance of the Protestant missionary and his Protestant Indians, who had come a journey of months to meet and assist their beloved teacher, and reached the Dalles of the Columbia, and the great emigrant route connecting the Atlantic and Pacific shores was established a sure thing, and became at once of the greatest national importance.

And 8th. By affording at the Protestant stations the yearly way-worn emigrants needed supplies of provisions in their long and often disastrous journey to reach this western wilderness, and at Dr. Whitman's an asylum for orphans who had lost parents and all on the route. Eleven adopted orphans were thus upon the hands of this philanthropist and his angel wife when they fell, and five of them mingled their blood with that of their adopted mother, who with her last breath was heard to pray— her heart's blood fast flowing out—"Oh! my dear Saviour, take care of my dear children, now to be left a second time orphans;" and in a whisper, "tell my mother for me that I fell at my post." And also stopping-places for many every year who were compelled to stop over winter on account of sickness, given-out teams, or the lateness of the season. Some fifty were thus wintering with the doctor when the massacre took place, and most of the men were butchered with the doctor. Again: in the Willamette Valley the Protestant stations were everywhere ready to greet their weary, broken-hearted, journey-stripped countrymen with needed supplies, shelter from Oregon storms, opportunity to labor, and with schools and with Christian society.

And 9. By furnishing the American people and the American Government the earliest and constant history of the extent and character of this great country in their numerous yearly journals and letters, which were published in the official journals of the respective mission boards, and in the newspapers of the day, and spread wide over the land.

And 10. By the steadfast devotion of the Protestant Nez Perces, the most powerful tribe west of the mountains, to the Americans and the American Government. Through that long and severe struggle to prevent or destroy the American settlements and annihilate Protestantism in Oregon; during the Whitman massacre, and the long wars that followed, till 1857, the Nez Perces—true to the teachings of their Protestant missionaries—remained constantly the firm allies and friends of the Americans, and opposing Indian sagacity to Indian sagacity, they were always the best allies of the Americans; the quickest to discover the designs of the enemy, and ready to strike at the critical moment. When the Jesuits and English had, by means of Indian runners, excited the surrounding tribes to butcher the Protestant missionaries and American emigrants at Waiilatpu and to exterminate the American settlements on the Pacific, the Nez Perces refused to join them, and first rushed at once to the defense of their beloved teacher, Mrs. Spalding, and rescued her and her infants from a band of forty of the murderers; then, second, fled to the scene of the eight days' carnage, and by their influence stopped the bloody work of the Jesuits; induced the Cayuses to give up the fifty Protestant women and children to Mr. Ogden; and themselves, third, brought Mr. Spalding and family safe through hostile tribes one hundred and fifty miles to Walla-Walla, and delivered them to Mr. Ogden, and when the Cayuse, urged on by the Jesuit Lewis, after they had obtained the ransom money, made the attempt to retake Mr. Spalding and the Americans, they threw themselves between them and beat them back till Mr. Ogden, by strong current and a most favorable wind, and the utmost nerve of every oarsman, was out of reach down the Columbia with his three boat-loads of human beings, mostly women and children, whom this true Protestant, through a kind Providence, had, almost as by miracle—no other man living could have saved them—rescued from the bloody tomahawk, or a fate worse than death; some of them in a dying state—all in a wretched condition; their husbands and fathers and brothers horribly butchered before their eyes; their flesh given to the beasts of the field; themselves subjected to horrors too shocking for the pen, and robbed of everything, and left destitute in a land of strangers.   But this is Romanism in Oregon: widows left with large families of young children, Dr. and Mrs. Whitman's large family of adopted orphans—left doubly orphans—without parents or relatives in the country. Some helpless children and their dying mothers were actually turned out by these Jesuits of one of the very establishments which the American Captain Mullan denominates "the St. Bernards of the West, where the weary traveler is always taken in and refreshed by the holy fathers," although he must have known its bloody record.

4. And again, in 1848, when all the tribes of the Northwest, under Jesuits, had assembled at Des Chutes, waiting for ammunition to be brought to them from the English post by the priests, with which to cut off the Willamette settlements and take their women and herds, had the Nez Perces joined them, as strongly urged, the last American family would have been butchered, as testifies Governor Abernathy, who ought to know; but they refused, and, on the other hand, sent word to the combined camp if they attempted to fall upon the American settlements they would fall upon their rear, sweep their country of their herds of horses, and retire east of the mountains. This unexpected intelligence coming at the moment of the unexpected seizure, by Lieutenant Rogers, of the ammunition from the priests, completely checked the savages, and saved the settlements, which, at the time, was peculiarly exposed, most of the men having rushed to the gold mines of California, and Romanism was again disappointed.

5. And again, in 1850, after the volunteers failed to apprehend the guilty Cayuse, the Nez Perces, at the request of the Government, rushed through the winter snows, overtook the savages on Upper John Day River, overcame the Cayuse in a long fight, killed some, and took five of their principal leaders and delivered them to the Government, and they were tried and executed at Oregon City.

6. Again, in 1855, when all the tribes of the Northwest were combined against the Americans, except the Nez Perces, as testifies Colonel Cornelius, had they joined the combination, (as they were sore pressed to do, thirty-seven oxen being killed at one feast to induce them to break their alliance with the Americans and join the combined hosts under the priests,) if the American settlements on this coast had not been broken up, they would have been involved in a most disastrous and expensive war.   But they steadily maintained their friendship to the Americans, as taught them by their missionaries; furnished provisions and cattle to our Army, express, to go where no white man could live; remounted our Army at one time with four hundred horses; at three different times furnished a battalion of warriors to aid our people when sore pressed by the combined hosts, who were constantly supplied with ammunition.

7. They flew to the rescue of Governor Stevens and party when their retreat was cut off, and when Colonel Steptoe was defeated in a two days' fight, one-fourth of his command killed or wounded, his retreat and water cut off and ammunition gone, which disaster was brought about by a treacherous Jesuit priest, acting the friend in the American camp, but really a spy for the savages, learning the colonel's small amount of ammunition, sent the savages word, and joined them as soon as the fight commenced with his packs of so-called groceries and nails, but really balls and powder.   Then it was Timothy, the Protestant, Nez Perces, preacher, and his two brothers, fighting with the Americans, discovering an unguarded opening in the rocks, taking advantage of the darkness and the uproar of the surrounding savages at their dance fires awaiting the dawn to scalp the last American, led out the colonel and his remnant, and, with the stillness of death, on through the night, to his country thus saved them and furnished them food.   And during all these years "we had to fight all the tribes which have been under Catholic priests," as reports Superintendent Nesmith, the Nez Perces, so thoroughly imbued with the principles of Protestantism and of the American Government that no hostile tribes nor Romish emissaries have been able to draw them from their allegiance, have remained a bulwark upon our frontiers, often preventing our settlements from being drenched in the blood of its citizens; and although, by the unwise policy of our Government, they have been deprived of the counsels and teachings of their old beloved mission for many long years, still they stand firm in their religion, and remain the most uncompromising friends of the American people, their constant

fidelity and friendship to the Americans being unanimously attributed by Superintendent Hale and Agents Anderson and Howe, long in charge of the tribe, by Governor Abernathy, General Palmer, and scores of miners and travelers, citizens and officers, both civil and military, and by about every religious lady in the State, to the long-continued and most successful labors and influence of the Rev. H. H. Spalding and his most amiable wife, now in Heaven.

Done by order of the Pleasant Bute Baptist Church, Brownsville, Linn County, Oregon, October 22, 1869.

H. I. C. AVERILL,
L. C. RICE,
H. R. POWELL,
Committee on Resolutions.
J. WARMOUTH,
Moderator.
J. A. C. AVERILL,
Clerk.

Done by order of the Christian Church at Brownsville, Oregon, this October 29, 1869.

JOHN M. HARRIS, *Moderator.*

Attest:

W. H. ROWLAND, *Clerk.*
OBADIAH THARP,
D. W. PUTMAN,
JOSEPH HUNTSAKER,
W. H. ROWLAND,
Committee.

Adopted unanimously at the annual meeting in Polk County, Oregon, Tuesday after third Sabbath in June, 1870, by the committee of the Brotherhood of the Christian Church in Oregon, and voted to be published in the Review at Cincinnati, and to be used by our beloved brother Spalding as he may deem proper, with as many of our names as may be necessary.

J. M. HARRIS, *Moderator.*
W. H. ROWLAND, *Clerk.*
WM. RUBLE and others, *Committee.*

THE OREGON MISSION AND THE UNITED STATES GOVERNMENT.

The undersigned committee, appointed by the Presbytery of Steuben to prepare and publish a report on what is known in history as the Oregon mission of the American Board of Commissioners for Foreign Missions, would earnestly call the attention of all concerned to the following facts and considerations:

1. Marcus Whitman, M. D., and Rev. H. H. Spalding, and their wives, missionaries of the A. B. C. F. M., were the first to prove that families could cross the American continent, by safely accomplishing that journey in 1836.

2. A successful mission was established by these pioneers among the Cayuse and Nez Perces Indians, in what was then known as the Oregon Territory. This was done by special permit of the United States Government. The mission was maintained eleven years, to the great benefit, as can be abundantly shown, of the Indians, especially of the large and powerful tribe of Nez Perces.

3. It is well known that then the whole of that northwest territory, though ostensibly in the joint occupancy of the United States and Great Britain, was really under the control of the Hudson's Bay Company. The agents of that British monopoly had driven away the last American trader from those shores, and were doing all in their power to exclude American settlers. Their efforts were so far successful, that, in the autumn of 1842, a treaty was about to be closed between the United States and Great Britain, transferring to the latter that whole territory.

4. It was at this important juncture that Dr. Whitman determined, notwithstanding the approach of winter, to cross the continent, and, if possible, save that country to the United States. A more hazardous undertaking, more heroically accomplished, the annals of adventure nowhere describe. That terrible winter journey, and its consequences, constitute a notable and thrilling chapter of our national history. Dr. Whitman reached Washington in the spring of 1843, barely in time to secure, by his representations of the country and the overland route, a postponement of the disastrous treaty until he should conduct an emigrant train to the Columbia River.

This task he accomplished during the following summer, bringing a train of one thousand souls safely through, thus completely demonstrating the feasibility of the overland route, and effectually securing that vast and valuable territory to the United States.

And from that time the mission station of Dr. Whitman at Waiilatpu was a well-known haven of rest and supplies to the emigrants passing through yearly to the Pacific coast.

5. It is, therefore, not surprising that the British officials in that region were greatly incensed against Dr. Whitman and his associates. It is now a matter of authentic history that extreme measures were soon resorted to by the agents of the Hudson's Bay Company to check the growth of American influence. Special agents from Europe appeared on the ground, and, by the aid of certain Roman Catholic priests, the Indians themselves were incited to violence by false reports concerning the missionaries, as, *e. g.*, that they had come to poison the Indians and possess their lands. The result of such intrigues was what might be expected. On the 29th of November, 1847, began the horrid Whitman massacre, in which Dr. Whitman and nineteen others were slain. Throughout those eight days of slaughter, Americans *only* were the victims. The priests and others who were there in the interests of the Hudson's Bay Company were unharmed, and there is every reason to believe that they only encouraged and assisted the savages in their bloody work. It was a white man that gave the signal for the slaughter to commence, and with his own hands he shot Mrs. Whitman. And the few who escaped were refused admittance at the forts of the company.

6. It is well known that the Whitman massacre was the beginning of an attempt to break up all American settlements in the Territory, and that the missionaries at the Lapwai station only escaped butchery through the friendly protection of the Nez Perces. There is also abundance of the best possible testimony from such men as Commodore Wilkes, United States Navy; Governor Abernathy, and General Joel Palmer; from many prominent United States officers, from missionaries, travelers, and citizens of the Territory, proving the fidelity to that mission of Mr. and Mrs. Spalding, and the great value to the United States Government of their labors among the Nez Perces. During the long and expensive war following the massacre, *this tribe alone*, among the Indians, was friendly to the Americans. And there is no doubt, as many have testified, that this was owing in a great measure to the teachings of Mr. Spalding; and, according to Mr. Anderson, several years agent of the Nez Perces, "Mr. Spalding by his own personal labors has accomplished more good to this tribe than all the money expended by the Government has been able to effect."

Having thus briefly alluded to the vast services rendered, and the almost unparalleled sufferings endured by the founders of the Oregon mission for their country, we pause to ask what has their country done for them. What has the General Government done in recognition of these services? How has the nation expressed its gratitude to the memory of those patriots, to whom we owe, under God, a large portion, if not all our possessions on the Pacific coast?

In the first place, a document bearing on this subject has been published by Congress, entitled "Executive Document No. 38, Thirty-fifth Congress, First Session," and containing ostensibly the report of J. Ross Browne as special agent of the Government to inquire into the causes of the Indian war in Oregon. But, on examination, we find this report, containing only twelve pages written by said Browne, and fifty-three other pages, made up of a pamphlet first published years before in New York City, by a Jesuit priest, Brouilette. But this pamphlet, it is plain, was prepared soon after the Whitman massacre, and is an attempt to screen the author and others from the charges brought against them of complicity in that tragedy. And there is overwhelming evidence of the best possible kind, that this portion of said congressional document contains many absolute falsehoods, and casts most infamous reflections upon Dr. Whitman and his associates. This Brouilette, it is proved, in part by his own testimony, was present at the massacre, doing nothing to save the victims, but baptizing the children of the murdering Indians, and otherwise stimulating them in their work of death. That such a man should have written such a pamphlet is not surprising. But why, we ask in the name of humanity and justice, why must Congress give currency to such slanders against the very men who achieved and suffered so much for their country? Why must the General Government give to so infamous and malignant an attack all the dignity and authority of an official document, and that, too, without publishing a scrap of the abundant rebutting testimony.

But this is not all. In another official document we find the Thirty-seventh Congress declaring that the Lapwai mission was "voluntarily abandoned" by the missionaries in December, 1847, which, as the world knows, is false and absurd. First driven away by the murdering savages of the Whitman massacre, the missionaries were afterward taken out of the country, and the country was closed against all missionaries by the Government until 1858.

And finally: "It is well known and proved that so soon as it was thought safe Mr. Spalding attempted to return, but was forbidden; and when he did and opened his schools among his old people, who were rejoiced to see him, and at once filled up church and school-room—as testified by Agent Anderson, these schools were broken up and himself forced from his old home, his orchards and buildings, his people and native (Indian) church," by the United States Government; nor has he since been permitted to return.

S. Ex. Doc. 37——6

Such, in its main features, has been and still is the attitude of the General Government toward the survivors of the Oregon mission! Such is almost the only recognition yet made by this nation of the invaluable services rendered by those martyred patriots and their associates!

We, therefore, in behalf of the Presbytery of Steuben, from whose bounds Dr. Marcus Whitman and Rev. H. H. Spalding went forth upon their mission in 1836; and firmly believing that the above statements are true, having ourselves examined much of the testimony referred to, do most earnestly unite with our fellow-citizens of the Pacific coast and the various Protestant churches there, in respectfully entreating Congress, as far as possible, to rectify the wrong done to the memory of the dead and the reputation of the living in the publication of the aforesaid Executive Document No. 38, Thirty-fifth Congress. To this end, we pray that a candid and well-attested account of the whole matter, about to be presented to Congress, may be published in a like official document.

We also, as a presbytery, would express our entire confidence in the high Christian character of these missionaries, who were well known to some of us personally. We especially hereby tender our warmest sympathies to our afflicted and faithful brother, Rev. H. H. Spalding.

We earnestly entreat of the Government at Washington that he may be restored to his beloved missionary work, and to the native church and schools which he was so successful in establishing.

And now, since the last Protestant missionary to the Indians beyond the Rocky Mountains has recently been driven from his field by the General Government, as is well known, and that, too, at the very time when the Government claims to be introducing a more humane and righteous Indian policy than has heretofore prevailed, we feel that, in common with all American Christians and all friends of humanity, we have the right to earnestly ask of our Government that this long series of grievous wrongs may cease, and these evils, so far as possible, be rectified.

By order of the Presbytery of Steuben:

D. HENRY PALMER,
JAMES H. HOTCHKIS,
O. F. MARSHALL,
Committee.

" Let not the country cast dishonor on unselfish patriotism.

" Let not the brand of infamy remain on the memory of the just.

"The publication of the allegations above mentioned by authority of Congress, doubtless through one of those inadvertencies which creep into the proceedings of deliberative bodies, calls for ample redress.

"We therefore unite with all patriotic and fair-dealing men in the earnest petition that the Congress of the United States should do justice to the memory of the dead and protect the rights of the living."

Adopted by the Oregon Presbytery, Old School Presbyterian Church.
A. L. LINDSLEY, D. D., *Moderator.*

Adopted also by the Oregon Presbytery, Cumberland Presbyterian Church.
W. R. BISHOP, *Moderator.*

Adopted also by the Oregon Presbytery, United Presbyterian Church.
I. DICK, *Moderator.*

Adopted also by the Oregon Conference Methodist Episcopal Church.
BISHOP KINGSLEY, *Moderator.*

Adopted also by the Oregon Congregational Association.
G. H. ATKINSON, D. D., *Moderator.*

Adopted also by the Pleasant Bute Baptist Church.
J. WARMOUTH, *Moderator.*

Adopted also at the annual meeting of the Oregon Christian Church.
JOHN HARRIS, *Moderator.*

And these bodies probably represent full 30,000 of the best inhabitants of the State. These sentiments are also concurred in by all the leading journals on this side of the mountains.

We have thus allowed the leading citizens of the State of Oregon and the Territory of Washington, and nearly all the Federal officers of the country, to speak for themselves on this all-important subject which the Congress of the United States, by their own vote, and in their own official documents, have placed in the hands of the people.

And now, with the utmost confidence, we commend these witnesses to that ever-watchful care over the truth of history, and to that sacred regard for unselfish patriotism which animates the bosom of every American.

H. H. SPALDING.

Assisted by—

Rev. W. H. ROWLAND.
Hon. R. H. CRAWFORD.
Hon. R. B. COCHRAN.
Hon. T. R. CORNELIUS.
Rev. J. S. GRIFFIN.
DUDLEY ALLEN, M. D.
JAMES H. HOTCHKIN, Esq.
E. R. GEARY, D. D.
Hon. I. R. MOORES.
Rev. J. M. HARRIS.
Rev. G. S. KENDALL.
J. C. H. AVERILL.
GUSTAVUS HINES, D. D.
JAMES BLACKESLY.
Rev. W. R. BISHOP.
G. H. ATKINSON, D. D.
Rev. LUTHER WHITE.
JOHN WILSON.

O

COLOPHON

This 1903 Senate Executive Document on the Whitman difficulties of 1847 was reprinted in the workshop of Glen Adams, which is located in the sleepy country village of Fairfield, southern Spokane County, in Washington State and one township removed from the Idaho line. Photography/darkroom work of the old pages was by Sylvia Fenich, using a 660C DS camera, and a LogE automatic film processing machine. Plates were made by David Hooper, who also printed the sheets using a model KORS Heidelberg press. Folding was by Garry Adams using a 22x28 three-stage Baum folding machine. The sheets were gathered and signatures assembled by Bonnie Cozzetto and Jessica La Tendresse. Paper stock is 70 pound Island Offset, a Canadian sheet. Binding is by Glen Adams and Garry Adams using a Mark II Sulby adhesive binding machine. This was a fun project. We had no special difficulty with the work.

Index